Absolute Legal English

Helen Callanan
and Lynda Edwards

DELTA Publishing
Quince Cottage
Hoe Lane
Peaslake
Surrey GU5 9SW
England

www.deltapublishing.co.uk

© Helen Callanan and Lynda Edwards 2010

The right of Helen Callanan and Lynda Edwards to be identified as authors of this work has been asserted by them in accordance with the Copyright, Designs and Patents Act, 1988.

All rights reserved. No reproduction, copy or transmission of this publication may be made without written permission from the publishers or in accordance with the provisions of the Copyright, Designs and Patents Act 1988, or under the terms of any licence permitting copying issued by the Copyright Licensing Agency, 90 Tottenham Court Road, London W1P 9HE.

First published 2010
Reprinted 2011, 2012

Edited by Catriona Watson-Brown
Designed by Caroline Johnston
Cartoons by Cartoonstock
Photos by iStock (page 88 a, d, e) and Shutterstock (page 88 b, c and page 92)
Cover design by Peter Bushell
Audio production by Ian Harker
Printed in China by RR Donnelley

ISBN 978-1-905085-51-4

Acknowledgments

The authors and publishers would like to thank the following for permission to reproduce copyright material:

Page 16: *What is fair?* adapted from www.lexnet.bravepages.co

Page 18: *Competition law* adapted from an article on Wikipedia

Page 26: *Competition law and sharing information among companies* adapted from www.out-law.com

Page 36 *Resolving employment disputes through mediation* adapted from an article by Michael J. Roberts

Page 39: *Drafting a commercial contract* adapted from www.wiwi.tu-treiberg.de

Page 40: *Enforceability of contracts* adapted from an article by Christopher Goddard

Page 46: *Buyers' terms and conditions and unfair contract terms* taken from www.businesslink.gov.uk

Page 50: *Online contractual transactions* adapted from an interview with Michael Geist in *International Trade Forum* magazine, issue 4/2002

Page 56: *Property law* adapted from an article on Wikipedia

Page 57: *If you are a property owner, then you can benefit from a lawyer's help* adapted from an article on www.nolo.com, reprinted with permission from the publisher, Nolo, copyright 2010, http://www.nolo.com

Page 62: *What are the pitfalls of buying property in Spain?* adapted from www.pinkfridge.com

Page 70: *Board meetings* adapted from www.out-law.com

Page 75: *Lawyer's involvement in maintaining a business entity* adapted from www.europeanrestructuring.com

Page 94: *Clinical legal education and environmental law* adapted from www.law.standford.edu

Every effort has been made to contact the copyright holders of the other texts reproduced in this book. The publishers will be happy to acknowledge them in future editions if they contact them at the address at the top of this page.

Contents

	Introduction	4
	About the ILEC exam	5
1	Intellectual property	10
2	Competition law	18
3	Employment law	28
4	Contract law 1 Drafting contracts	38
5	Contract law 2 Enforceability of contracts, breach of contract and remedies	48
6	Real property law	56
7	Company law 1 Business entities: types and requirements	64
8	Company law 2 Business entities: maintenance, expansion and conclusion	72
9	Environmental law	86
	Audio transcripts	96
	Answer key	105
	Glossary	111

Introduction

Absolute Legal English (ALE) is a book designed for both students of law and practising lawyers who wish to improve their level of English. It is suitable for those who wish to work in an international legal environment and need to extend their language skills to be able to read and understand English in a legal context and to communicate effectively, both orally and in writing.

ALE provides practice in all language skills and uses a variety of legal text types and situations to provide stimuli for tasks and to develop a range of vocabulary, including collocations, phrasal verbs, word formation, and formal and informal equivalents. Many sections of the units give integrated skills practice by developing a thematic link, so language is frequently recycled in different contexts. Many tasks also help develop certain legal skills at the same time as giving linguistic practice. Tasks which are specifically aimed at developing language are flagged as 'Language work'. There are also tasks which require students to do further research on one of the topics of the unit; these are flagged as 'Research' and could be set for homework in a classroom-based context.

ALE will help prepare students who wish to take the ILEC examination. The final two pages of each unit provide practice in task types from each of the four papers, all related to the topic of the unit, and there is a useful exam tip with each task. An overview of the ILEC examination follows this introduction.

ALE covers the main legal areas studied in International law, and at the end of the book there is a short glossary of additional useful terms not specifically covered in the units, relating to the sale of goods, supplies of services, negotiable instruments, secured transactions and legal Latin. *ALE* is aimed at students who are studying in either the United Kingdom or their own countries. The answers to the tasks and transcripts of recordings are all at the back of the book, so *ALE* is equally appropriate for use in class or for self-study.

About the ILEC exam

What is ILEC?

ILEC is an internationally accepted examination which provides a high-level qualification for lawyers. It assesses language skills within a legal context and provides proof of the level of English required to work in an international legal context and to follow a course of study at university level. It is therefore an ideal qualification for both students of law and those who have already worked in the legal profession in their own countries.

ILEC stands for International Legal English Certificate and is a Cambridge ESOL examination set at Levels B1 and B2 of the Common European Framework. These are equivalent in level to the Cambridge First Certificate in English (FCE) and the Certificate in Advanced English (CAE).

ILEC is recognized by many legal associations and bodies worldwide.

What does the ILEC exam consist of?

The ILEC exam is divided into four tests, and a candidate's final grade is based on the total score achieved over all four tests. This means that it is possible to compensate for a weak result in one test by doing well in another. Each test accounts for 25% of the final mark. The tests are:

- Reading Test
- Writing Test
- Listening Test
- Speaking Test

All the tests are based on realistic tasks, topics and materials that practising lawyers would expect to deal with in their daily working lives. The exam does not test knowledge of the law itself, but the language skills necessary to communicate in a legal context. Therefore, candidates should be familiar with certain legal concepts and the terminology associated with international commercial law.

READING TEST (1 hour 15 minutes)

The Reading Test has six different parts:
- Part 1: Multiple-choice cloze (12 questions)
- Part 2: Open cloze (12 questions)
- Part 3: Word formation (12 questions)
- Part 4: Multiple matching (6 questions)
- Part 5: Gapped text (6 questions)
- Part 6: Multiple choice (6 questions)

Part 1: Multiple-choice cloze

There are two short gapped texts, and each is followed by a set of four-option multiple-choice items. Candidates choose the best word to fill each gap. This task type mainly tests vocabulary, collocations, fixed phrases, linking expressions, etc. The words presented in the options are usually close in meaning, so students often need to consider structural fit and collocation to find the correct word.

Part 2: Open cloze

This consists of one gapped text. Candidates supply the best word to fill each gap. The focus here is mainly on structural knowledge, and students will need to supply items such as articles, auxiliaries, conjunctions, prepositions, etc. The correct answer will depend on and relate to the structure and meaning of the sentence and be appropriate to the overall meaning of the text. It is useful to use the context of the sentence to decide which part of speech you are looking for. Only one word per gap is ever required.

Part 3: Word formation

There are two short gapped texts, and students have to form an appropriate word from a base word that is given. This may involve prefixes, suffixes, changing from noun to adjective, etc. To be successful in this part of the test, candidates need to have a good basic knowledge of word families. Again, candidates should try to identify the word class of the item they have to form from the context.

Part 4: Multiple matching

This consists of either one long text divided into four sections or four short texts. Candidates match questions with the relevant sections. This test demands a good understanding of the meaning of a text and the ability to locate specific information. Students should be aware that the information from the text will be paraphrased in the questions and not match word for word.

Part 5: Gapped text

The difference between this part and other parts with gapped texts is that here sentences, not single words, have been removed from the text. The sentences are listed (with an additional sentence which serves as a distractor), and candidates have to identify which sentences go where in the text. This part tests candidates' understanding of the overall meaning and structure of the text; to find the correct sentence for each gap, candidates need to look at both the meaning and structure of the previous and following sentences in the text. It is often useful to consider linking expressions and reference devices.

Part 6: Multiple choice

For this part of the test, candidates read a complete text and then answer questions about it. Each question has four possible answers. To find the correct answers, candidates need to understand the text very well and differentiate between subtle and often similar opinions, reasons or results expressed in it. Candidates need to remember that there will be distraction in the text. This means that there will be some information in the text that links with the wrong options. It is a good idea to read the whole text through before looking at the questions.

WRITING TEST (1 hour 15 minutes)

The Writing Test has two parts. Both are compulsory.
- Part 1: a letter (120–180 words) (40% of the marks)
- Part 2: a memorandum (200–250 words) (60% of the marks)

The letter

Candidates have to write a response to an input letter and five content points. A situation involving law-related issues will be outlined in the question, and candidates read part of a letter related to this situation with accompanying notes. They must address all of these notes when writing the responding letter. The notes will cover certain functions, e.g. *Don't agree – say why!* (explaining); *Arrange a date to discuss* (suggesting); *That's wrong – say why!* (correcting). There are many points to consider when writing this letter. Candidates must give themselves enough time to read the input material thoroughly and plan their letter to include *all* the points in the notes. The task is designed for candidates to expand on the points given, and those who simply 'lift' whole phrases from the input material will be penalized. Candidates should try to reformulate rather than copy, using their own words.

Candidates must also consider an appropriate style – this will usually be formal – and use appropriate letter-writing conventions – opening, paragraphing and closing phrasing. Marks are given for organization and cohesion (sentence linking and using discourse markers), layout and accuracy, as well as range of structures and vocabulary. Planning, drafting and checking are therefore all important.

The memorandum (memo)

For this task, candidates are given a situation which requires them to write a detailed memo. They need to imagine that they work in a law firm and have to write a memo to a colleague. It may be that they are going on a break and have to pass their case load to a colleague. This could involve them giving details related to a particular case. Another common scenario is that a colleague has asked for advice on what to include in a presentation he/she has to make. Candidates are given points that they must address in the memo (such as outlining the case, explaining what has been done so far, what problems to look out for) or points to include in a talk and reasons, etc. It is very important once again to address all the points given in the input.

This task allows candidates to be more creative with ideas and language. They should use their imagination or experience of real cases or situations to give authenticity to the memo. For example, if the memo is about two companies that are merging, candidates should give names to the companies and invent relevant data.

Candidates will be marked as before on their task achievement, and special focus will be given to the range of structures and vocabulary used, as well as grammatical accuracy.

LISTENING TEST (40 minutes)

The Listening Test is divided into four parts:
- Part 1: Multiple choice: three short monologues or dialogues (6 questions)
- Part 2: Multiple choice: one dialogue between two or more people (5 questions)
- Part 3: Sentence completion: one monologue (9 questions)
- Part 4: Multiple matching: five themed monologues (10 questions)

Part 1: Multiple choice

Candidates listen to three short monologues or dialogues which are unrelated. For each of these, they have to answer two three-option multiple-choice questions. Candidates are given a sentence on the question paper to contextualize the extract before they start to listen. The questions test understanding of gist, detail, opinion, inference, function and topic. Candidates may find that it is better to focus on the question stems rather than trying to read and remember all options before hearing the extracts.

Part 2: Multiple choice

Candidates hear one longer conversation between two or more speakers on a legal issue and answer five three-option multiple-choice questions. These test understanding of gist, specific information, opinion and attitude. This is the longest part of the listening test, and candidates need to follow the conversation closely to hear when it moves on or changes direction. The questions will always be given in order, and candidates can use the questions to guide them through while they are listening. Many of the questions in this part will paraphrase and/or report ideas and points that come up in the conversation. Therefore candidates should be familiar with reporting verbs such as *recommends, suggests, complains*, etc.

Part 3: Sentence completion

This task involves filling gaps in sentences with words from a monologue. On the question paper, candidates will have a gapped summary or paraphrase of information given in the recording. The words they need to complete the information will be exactly the same words they hear, so they do not need to paraphrase or change the wording, and there will usually be no more than three words needed for each gap. Once again, the information required is in the same order as the candidates hear it. It is important to read the sentences very carefully before listening to the extract, as this will help in several ways. Firstly, it will give candidates a clear idea of what the extract is about. Secondly, it will indicate what they are listening for at each point. Thirdly, it is useful for predicting what type of word(s) they are listening for, e.g. a noun, a name, a place, etc. Most questions will require concrete information such as this. Another useful point to remember is that the information required to complete the sentences will be introduced in some way in the recording, and candidates should listen for clues as to when the answers are coming up. For example, with a gap that requires a particular date, the recording might have *The dates for this year's awards have just been announced. They will be held on the …* Candidates should be sure that what they have written fits logically and grammatically into the sentence.

Part 4: Multiple matching

In this part of the test, candidates listen to five speakers and have to identify topics, functions, attitude or opinion. There will be two tasks to do from the same recordings, with five questions for each task. The five short monologues are related to each other by theme and are heard in a sequence. Candidates are then given time to do the first matching task before listening to the whole sequence again to do the second. This task mainly tests listening for gist, so candidates do not have to understand or remember specific information. The prospect of having to do two tasks from the same recording can sometimes worry candidates, but as long as they treat each task separately, it is quite straightforward. They should also attempt to make predictions about the kinds of attitudes and ideas they might expect to hear in connection with the topic before they listen.

SPEAKING TEST (16 minutes)

The Speaking Test is taken by pairs of candidates. Occasionally, candidates may be in threes, but never alone. In the test, there will be one examiner (the interlocutor) who asks the questions and another who assesses the candidates' language.

There are four parts:
- Part 1: Introductory questions
- Part 2: Individual long turn
- Part 3: Collaborative task
- Part 4: Related questions and discussion

Part 1: Introductory questions
At the beginning of the test, the interlocutor asks both candidates some general questions about their legal studies or work and their opinions on general law-related issues. These questions are intended to relax the candidates and start them talking easily; they should not be too difficult to answer.

Part 2: Individual long turn
In this part of the test, candidates have to talk for a minute about one particular topic. In turn, candidates are given a booklet with a choice of two topics to talk about. With each topic, there are suggestions of what to include in the talk should the candidates wish to use them. Each candidate has a minute to read through the topics carefully, decide which to talk about and think of some ideas. There is no opportunity to make notes. The interlocutor will ask which topic has been chosen, and the candidate then talks for a minute. The other candidate listens and has to ask his/her partner a question about the talk. The process is then repeated with the second candidate. Candidates must try to link ideas well to give a balanced talk that is easy to follow. It does not matter whether or not they use all the prompts given. What is important is that they continue to talk on the topic for a minute. Candidates should remember that a minute is quite a short time!

Part 3: Collaborative task
Candidates do this part of the test together. They are given a situation and have to discuss what to do. For example, they may have to decide what advice to give a client. They have three minutes for the task. Again, there are prompts to help them, but they do not have to use them. It is important that the candidates interact with each other and do not simply take turns to give their ideas.

Part 4: Related questions and discussion
The interlocutor asks candidates in turn questions related to and developing the theme of the previous task. These often involve giving an opinion. It is usually a good idea for candidates to develop their answers rather than give a simple, one-sentence answer, as this part of the test is a good opportunity for candidates to show their range of language and ability to discuss topics in depth. The second candidate may be invited to comment on the first candidate's response, so that this stage of the test becomes a mini-discussion.

1 Intellectual property

■ **Lead-in** | **Discuss these questions with a partner.**
1 What is intellectual property?
2 How can intellectual property be protected?
3 What particular problems are there in protecting intellectual property today?

Reading

1 Read the first paragraph of an article about intellectual property below and answer these questions.
1 What two reasons are given for ensuring intellectual property protection?
2 What are the two legal categories mentioned?
3 Why does the article mention these two categories?

Domestic legislation enacted within countries ensures intellectual property protection for two reasons: firstly, to give statutory expression to the moral and economic rights of creators in their creations and to the rights of the public in accessing those creations; and secondly, to promote creativity and the dissemination and application of the results and to encourage fair trade, thereby contributing to social and economic development. The division of intellectual property into two distinct legal categories, namely industrial property and copyright, results in different rights, duties and obligations, giving rise to varying degrees of protection and enforcement.

2 Explain the difference between *rights*, *duties* and *obligations*. Give an example of each.

3 Find words and phrases in the paragraph that mean the same as these.
1 encourage   2 separate   3 causes   4 legal   5 passed   6 which are

4 Decide whether these terms relate to industrial property or copyright.
commercial names   designations   disclosure   infringement
layout designs   licence   patents   performance   register
reproduction   trademarks   translation

5 Read the rest of the article on the next page to check your answers to Exercise 4.

6 Read the whole article again and answer these questions.
1 What is the difference between the expressions *authors' rights* and *copyright*?
2 Does an invention have to exist to be protected?
3 Why does the duration of protection for industrial property and copyright differ?
4 How is the public made aware that an invention is protected?
5 Why is there no need for a register of copyright?

Industrial property, in broad terms, protects inventions and includes patents to protect inventions and industrial designs. In addition, it covers trademarks, service marks, layout designs of integrated circuits, commercial names and designations, as well as geographical indications and protection against unfair competition.

Copyright, also known as authors' rights in most European languages, relates to artistic creations, such as books, music, paintings and sculptures, and films and technology-based works, such as computer programs and electronic databases. While the expression *copyright* refers to the main act, that act is the making of copies of the work, whereas the expression *authors' rights* relates to the creator of the artistic work, namely its author. The author has certain specific rights in his creation which only he can exercise, such as the right to prohibit or authorize its reproduction, distribution, performance, communication to the public, translation or adaptation, and these are recognized in most laws. Other rights, such as the right to make copies, can be exercised by other persons where permission or a licence has been obtained from the author. A created work is regarded as protected as soon as it comes into existence. Copyright ensures the protection of the authors' rights and provides remedies for the author in the event of any infringement.

Essentially, copyright protects the form of expression of ideas, whereas in the context of industrial property, inventions can be considered as new solutions to technical problems, and these solutions are ideas and are protected as such. In fact, protection of inventions under patent law does not require the invention to be actually physically in existence. The difference between inventions and literary and artistic works gives rise to different degrees of legal protection. As protection for inventions gives a monopoly over the right to exploit an idea, the duration of such protection is usually about 20 years, which is quite short. On the other hand, the protection of literary and artistic works prevents unauthorized use of the expression of the ideas, so the duration of the protection can be much longer. Furthermore, the public must be made aware of the fact that the invention is protected, and this is done publicly through disclosure in an official register, whereas a created work is considered protected as soon as it exists, and a public register of copyrights is not required.

7 Complete these phrases with words from both sections of the article.

1 in broad _____
2 _____ an idea
3 obtain a _____
4 two _____ legal categories
5 make someone _____ of the fact that ...
6 _____ to different degrees of protection

Language work

8 What are the verbs that relate to these nouns? Mark the stressed syllable in each word.

1 competition   2 permission   3 remedy   4 monopoly
5 solution   6 disclosure

9 Work in pairs. Each of you should talk for one minute about your subject. After each talk, your partner will ask you a question about it.

Student A: The need for intellectual property to be protected

Student B: The legal situation regarding protection of intellectual property in your country

> **USEFUL LANGUAGE**
>
> I should like to start by mentioning ...
> To begin with, I must say that ...
> We must also consider ...
> An important point regarding ... is ...
> There are many points to consider.
>
> Firstly, ... secondly, ... finally, ...
> I should also point out that ...
> Following on from that, ...
> I should add that ...
> In conclusion, ...

Research

10 Find out about the problems involved in protecting intellectual property on the Internet and discuss in class.

Listening

'This call may be monitored for training purposes or just to keep our staff amused.'

1 Imagine that a new client contacts you by phone. Rank these responses 1–5 according to what you would generally do (1 = never, 5 = always).

1 Listen sympathetically and advise a meeting.
2 Give advice over the telephone.
3 Immediately put the client through to your secretary to make an appointment.
4 Tell the client your hourly rate at the beginning of the conversation.
5 Ask the client to write out the problem with the facts and send it to you.

2 Work in pairs. Discuss the reasons for your ranking.

3 Would your response change according to the type of problem the client has, or who the client is? How?

4 1.1 Listen to a telephone conversation between a lawyer, Mr Howard, and a new client, Professor Daykin. Decide whether these statements are true or false.

1 Mr Howard has met Professor Daykin before.
2 Professor Daykin is upset because she has been cheated.
3 The conversation is angry.

5 1.1 Listen again and answer these questions.

1 How does Professor Daykin know Mr Howard?
2 Why doesn't Professor Daykin want to make an appointment?
3 Why have the course packs been put together, and what do they contain?
4 What have the authors given their permission for?
5 Who is Professor Daykin angry with, and why?
6 What does Mr Howard think should happen next? Why?

Language work

6 a Match the verbs in the left column (1–8) with the words and phrases in the right column (a–h) to make collocations from the conversation.

1 give   a it at that
2 get   b me know
3 go   c a quick outline
4 talk   d in touch
5 let   e into the matter
6 look   f it through
7 leave   g ahead
8 be   h back to you

b Who uses each of the above collocations, Mr Howard (H) or Professor Daykin (D)? Read the audio transcript on page 96 to check.

c Write five sentences using five of the collocations above. Remove the collocations to create gap-fill sentences for your partner to complete.

7 Read the audio transcript on page 96 and underline eight words you would like to check the meanings of. Compare your words with your partner's. Can you explain any? Use your dictionary for the other meanings.

1 Intellectual property

Speaking 1

1 Work in pairs. Practise reading these extracts from the conversation in the previous section.

> I feel at this stage that you should write out in detail what you've told me and send it to me so that I can look into the matter further and get back to you. I have the gist of it, but I would need to look at it much more carefully. I can certainly understand how you feel. The quicker we deal with it the better.

> That's excellent. I'll get down to it right now, and maybe you could give me a call when you've had a chance to look at it.

> That sounds perfect. Now, if you'll excuse me, we'll have to leave it at that for now. I'll be in touch as soon as possible, Professor. Goodbye for now.

Language work

2 a Decide whether these expressions are used to advise (A), explain (E) or show concern (SC).

1. I'm really worried about …
2. What happened was …
3. I think the next step is to …
4. The main points are as follows: …
5. In your position, I would …
6. I really don't know what to do.
7. I think we should look at …
8. It's like this.
9. I feel at this stage you should …
10. I'm afraid that …

b Work in pairs. Think of a way to complete or follow each expression.

3 Work in pairs. Role-play a conversation between a lawyer and a new client about an intellectual property problem.

Student A

You are a lawyer and you are talking on the telephone with a new client, Student B.
- Listen to his/her problem.
- Reassure him/her.
- Ask questions.
- Encourage him/her to give as much detail as possible.
- Pause appropriately.
- Make suggestions.
- Give whatever advice you feel is needed in the circumstances.

Student B

You are a client and you have phoned your lawyer, Student A, because you have just found out that some of the notes that you give to your students have been copied by a student and are being sold for a profit on the university campus.
- Give your reasons for being upset and worried.
- Explain the problem.
- Inform your lawyer that you have spoken to the student involved, but that he denies the copying and selling.
- Ask what you should do next.
- Say that you worry about making false accusations; this might affect your relationship with other students.

Writing

1 Discuss these questions in groups.

1 How strong do you think Professor Daykin's case is? Why?
2 What do you think Mr Howard will do next? Why?

2 a Without looking at the audio transcript, summarize Professor Daykin's problem orally in one minute.

b Read the letter below from Professor Daykin. Did your summary include all the points in the letter?

c Read the letter again and complete the gaps using the words and phrases in the box.

already	as well as	concerned	following this	further
	furthermore	hear	recently	sincerely

Dear Mr Howard,

I am writing to you **(1)** _____ to our telephone conversation today. Five-Star Document Services is a copy shop and provides general photocopy reproduction services to the general public **(2)** _____ to students of Sarvat University. Some of its profits come from the sale of course packs to students.

The course packs are a compilation of various copyrighted and uncopyrighted materials selected by the professors involved in the different courses. We all have an agreement with Sarvat University Press. They process requests for publishing our copyrighted materials and other materials and look after payment of the royalties or permission fees. **(3)** _____ , the materials are given to Five-Star Document Services with an estimate of the number of students expected on the course. The course packs are only sold to the students on a particular course and are not for sale to the general public.

(4) _____ , Five-Star Document Services made multiple copies of a pack that I had compiled and sold them to the general public. I and other professors hold the copyright to several excerpts which were included in the pack. **(5)** _____ , a number of journal articles, newspaper articles, course notes, syllabi, sample questions and excerpts were also included. I have **(6)** _____ spoken to the manager of Five-Star Document Services, and he has told me that as far as he is **(7)** _____ , their actions are legitimate. This whole matter is very embarrassing and particularly upsetting for me, as my reputation is at stake.

I hope to **(8)** _____ from you soon.

Yours **(9)** _____

Professor Daykin

1 Intellectual property

3 Mr Howard is going to write a letter to Five-Star Document Services (FSDS). Here are some of the points he is going to include. Put them in the correct order for the letter.

a proposed action
b warning about number of authors affected
c who he is representing
d the damage FSDS's actions could cause
e outline of the background
f how FSDS has broken the agreement
g action already taken

Language work

4 Which of the expressions in the box below could you use when writing about points a–g in Exercise 3?

> **USEFUL LANGUAGE**
> In relation to …
> One of the terms provides that …
> We are instructed that …
> Our client has suffered …
> We will be left with no alternative but to …
> This is covered by …
> The terms and conditions specifically provide …
> Our client informs us that …
> Alternatively, …
> It is our intention to …
> We require you to …
> It may well be that …
> You will be liable for …
> On behalf of …
> Your response was …

5 Work in pairs. Discuss how you would group the points into paragraphs and what information you would include.

6 Write the letter from Mr Howard to Five-Star Document Services. Use this checklist to help you.
- Divide your letter into clear paragraphs.
- Use the correct register.
- Make use of all the information in your notes.
- Link sentences.
- Check grammar and spelling.

Speaking 2

1 How do you think Five-Star Document Services will respond? Why? Use these beginnings to give your opinions in pairs.

2 Give your opinions in full group. Do you agree with your classmates' ideas? Why (not)?

1 Intellectual property

Reading: Part 1

TIP
Read the whole gapped text first to get a general understanding of it. See if you can predict any of the words before looking at the choices.

Read this extract from an article about fair use and complete each of the gaps with the best word: A, B, C or D.

What is fair?

A **(0)** _major_ exception to the presumption of copyright is the 'fair-use' doctrine. Like copyright, fair use is based on an economic **(1)**_____ in that fair use exists to remedy a market failure, whereas new technologies make mass copying inexpensive and represent a potential market failure. The fair-use doctrine can be **(2)**_____ from a purely economic perspective in that when the benefit to society of breach of the author's monopoly **(3)**_____ the benefit to society of the author's monopoly plus the benefit to the author of that monopoly, the information may be used, despite the fact that it would **(4)**_____ be the monopoly of the author.

The fair-use doctrine is both more necessary and more **(5)**_____ in contemporary global markets than it was in the past when the markets were mainly national and copying was costly. The cost of copying material is now **(6)**_____ zero because of the availability of new technologies, as is the cost of **(7)**_____ of the information. Information can now be diffused globally at almost no cost at all. This is in fact common **(8)**_____ in the use of the Internet when images or sounds are downloaded or uploaded, sometimes edited, sometimes commented on and sometimes **(9)**_____ back to their original source or to other works. Are such derived works permissible? According to the fair-use doctrine, Internet authors who 'borrow' images without **(10)**_____ but then link back the images to the original source would be more likely to be **(11)**_____ fair users. **(12)**_____ the source and/or advertising the source can weigh in favour of the finding of a use 'fair'.

0	A big	B major	C large	D great
1	A reason	B idea	C logic	D foundation
2	A angled	B watched	C pictured	D viewed
3	A disadvantages	B balances	C outweighs	D overcomes
4	A alternatively	B otherwise	C besides	D also
5	A conflicting	B contentious	C discussed	D worrying
6	A approaching	B reaching	C becoming	D getting
7	A spread	B circulation	C scattering	D posting
8	A exercise	B activity	C practice	D form
9	A related	B linked	C connected	D joined
10	A allowance	B decision	C acceptance	D permission
11	A considered	B signified	C seen	D described
12	A Claiming	B Denoting	C Citing	D Exemplifying

Speaking: Part 2

TIP
Try to include reference to all three points. If you're not sure what to say about one, leave it out and talk about the other two. You won't be penalized. The important thing is to keep talking for one minute.

Look at these two topics. Select one of them and give a short talk on it for about a minute. There are some ideas to help you. You have a minute to prepare your talk. After you have finished your talk, your partner will ask you a brief question about it.

TASK 1
Dealing with new clients
- Making a good impression
- Gaining the client's trust
- Clarifying procedures

TASK 2
Copyright
- Difficulties in establishing ownership
- How copyright can be infringed
- Remedies for copyright infringement

1 Intellectual property

Listening: Part 3

🎧 **3** **1.2** You will hear part of a talk about registered design protection. For questions 1–9, complete the notes.

TIP
You'll hear the words you need to complete the notes, but the notes themselves are always phrased differently to what you hear. Read the gapped notes first so that you have an idea what information you're going to listen for.

★ It is possible to buy designs that have been illegally (1) _____ in the high street.

★ Today, the people making the imitations are (2) _____ and _____ than they used to be.

★ In the past, designers have usually accepted that copying is (3) _____ in the fashion industry.

★ Top Shop was prosecuted by a (4) _____ fashion house, Chloe.

★ Jimmy Choo took action because a (5) _____ and a _____ design were copied.

★ Out-of-court settlement is common in most cases because those involved don't want to (6) _____ _____ .

★ Registered Design Protection (RDP) is simple and (7) _____ to apply for.

★ RDP protects designs for jewellery, (8) _____ and _____ as well as clothes.

★ RDP only applies to designs that have been registered before being shown in (9) _____ .

Writing: Part 2

TIP
Make sure you include all the points in your memo, even if some have more detail than others, otherwise you'll lose marks.

You are leaving your law firm to spend six months working abroad and are transferring your case load to a colleague. A client, a famous fashion house, is involved in a dispute with a high-street chain store regarding the copying of some of its designs.

Write a memorandum to your colleague to brief him on the case. Include these points:
- some background information about the case
- what action has been taken so far
- what future legal action can be taken
- what the immediate next steps are.

Write your answer in 200–250 words in an appropriate style.

1 Intellectual property

2 Competition law

■ Lead-in

Discuss these questions with a partner.

1 What do you know about competition law?
2 Can you name and talk about any recent famous cases in your country?

Reading 1

1 Answer these questions, then read the article below to check your answers.

1 Competition law monitors two main types of commercial activity. What are they?
2 What is competition law known as in the USA?
3 Is a knowledge of competition law only important for big businesses?
4 What can the consequences of breaching competition law be for:
   a businesses   b individuals?
5 What are the two main systems of competition law?

COMPETITION LAW

Competition law essentially prohibits agreements or practices that restrict free trading or competition between business entities. It also bans abusive behaviour by a firm dominating a market or anticompetitive practices that lead to a dominant position, such as predatory pricing, tying, price gouging and refusal to deal. In the United States, it is known as antitrust law, because trusts could be set up which businesses could hide behind and behave in a way that could be anticompetitive.

Competition law is designed on the one hand to enhance and on the other hand to regulate all forms of commercial and business transactions. As such, any business, whatever its legal status, size and sector, needs to be aware of competition law for many reasons. Firstly, so that it can meet its obligations and, in so doing, avoid findings where agreements are unenforceable. Secondly, to remove the risk of being fined up to 10% of group global turnover for particularly damaging behaviour. Thirdly, in order to remove the possibility of possible damages actions from customers. Fourthly, to minimize the risk of individuals in business facing director disqualification orders or even criminal sanctions for serious breaches of competition law; and fifthly, so that it can assert its rights and enable it to protect its position in the marketplace. The two largest and most influential systems of competition law regulation are the United States antitrust law and the European Community competition law. While there has been a tendency for international competition law to follow the model of the United States, there have been developments internationally involving nation states. Frameworks to shape competition policy and the effects of monopolies and cartels are developed by the United Nations Conference on Trade and Development (UNICTAD), the Organization for Economic Co-operation and Development (OECD) and the World Trade Organisation (WTO), together with the International Competition Network (ICN).

Language work

2 Find nouns or noun phrases in the article that collocate with these verbs.

1 restrict
2 dominating
3 set up
4 meet
5 avoid
6 remove
7 minimize
8 assert
9 protect

3 a Match these words to make collocations from the article.

1 abusive
2 price
3 group global
4 business
5 criminal
6 disqualification
7 predatory
8 anticompetitive
9 damages

a sanctions
b pricing
c behaviour
d practices
e gouging
f actions
g turnover
h entities
i orders

b Write a sentence using each collocation in context.

c Work in pairs. Test your partner on the collocations by giving the first or second part to elicit the other.

4 Complete these sentences with *so* or *such*.

1 The company provides training sessions _____ that its employees can keep up to date with new legislation.
2 The company agreed to keep its prices high and, in _____ doing, it contravened the law.
3 There are many consequences of breaching this particular law, _____ as a very large fine.
4 _____ behaviour is considered abusive.
5 The legislation was _____ difficult to interpret that it needed clarification.

5 Work in pairs. Take it in turns to choose one of the words in the box and define or describe it for your partner to guess. When they have guessed the word, they must put it into a sentence of their own.

| a trust | ban | breach | damages | disqualification | dominate |
| enhance | fined | influential | prohibit | restrict | unenforceable |

'Would it be more economical for them to develop their own comparable product or steal the competition's formula and fight it out in the courts?'

2 Competition law

Reading 2

1 Discuss these questions with a partner.

1 What is the difference between making a *presumption* about X and something that is *deemed* to be X?
2 What are the two meanings of the word *undertaking*?
3 What do you understand by the term *dominant undertaking*?

2 You are going to read about the criteria used by some different countries to determine whether an undertaking is dominant. Scan the summaries on the opposite page and answer these questions.

1 Which countries do not have a statutory threshold?
2 Which countries do each of these percentages relate to? What exactly do the percentages refer to?

a 5%   b 30%   c 35%   d 40%   e 40/50%   f 50%   g 80%

3 Read the summaries again carefully and say in which country competition law does the following.

1 defines other elements for consideration in determining dominance
2 has two statutory provisions
3 looks at dominance from a different angle
4 requires an undertaking to be one of four major players

Research

4 Do you know the situation in your country? Research the situation in three other countries and tell the class.

> **USEFUL LANGUAGE**
> … must not exceed …
> … must be lower than …
> … must have a joint market share of …
> … must be greater than …
> … must be equal to …
> … must make up at least …

'Well, *now* it's been explained to you. "Market share" does not mean we want to share the market.'

Austria

Section 4, sub-section 2 of the Austrian Cartel Act 2005 provides that an undertaking bears the burden of proof to show it is not dominant on the relevant market if the undertaking (a) has a market share of above 30%, or (b) has a market share of more than 5% provided that it is exposed to competition of not more than two other competitors, or has a market share of more than 5% and belongs to the four biggest undertakings on the relevant market which have a joint market share of at least 80%.

Belgium

There is no statutory market share threshold contained in the Competition Act, but case law suggests that there is a presumption of dominance if there is a market share of 50% or more.

Bulgaria

Article 17, paragraph 2 of the Bulgarian Protection of Competition Act provides that any undertaking is deemed to be dominant if its market share exceeds 35%.

Cyprus

Under the Protection of Competition Law, no market share threshold is defined. The Act focuses on what constitutes an abuse of a dominant position, rather than what is a dominant undertaking.

Czech Republic

Article 10 of the Competition Act states that an undertaking shall be deemed not to be in a dominant position if its share in the relevant market does not exceed 40% unless otherwise proven by indices specified in the articles. These indices include the volume of sales or purchases in the relevant market, the economic and financial power of the undertaking, the legal or other barriers of entry into the market by other undertakings, the level of vertical integration of the undertakings, the market structure and the market shares of immediate competitors.

France

The Commercial Code or the case law of the Competition Council do not set a threshold of dominance. A market share of above 40/50% may be considered as a factor, but this is not the only element taken into account by the Competition Council when analyzing the existence of a dominant position. In addition, market shares are not always the main basis for a decision.

Listening

1 Discuss these questions with a partner.
1 What is a legal elements chart? How can it help lawyers?
2 What would you expect to find in a legal elements chart?
3 What is the difference between *elements* and *factual propositions*?

2 In which section of a legal elements chart would these statements be included, elements (E), factual propositions (FP) or fact (F)?
1 Article 81 forbids agreements between undertakings […] which have as their object or effect to prevent, restrict or distort within the common market.
2 X Distributors, based in Austria, and Y Distributors, based in Finland, agreed to import and to sell Zozo cars at the same price in both countries at a price 10% cheaper than Zozo cars in all other EU states.
3 Mrs Jones bought a Zozo car in Austria 10% cheaper than in any other EU country.
4 Article 81 provides that an undertaking is every entity engaged in economic activity regardless of its legal status and how it is financed.
5 Three Internet providers based in Belgium, Germany and France offer broadband at the same price in the three countries.
6 One company, based in Spain, whose director was a director of all three Internet providers in question in Belgium, Germany and France, used this Internet provider for his business in Spain.
7 State-owned corporations or the state itself may be controlled by EU competition law if they or it act as private undertakings.
8 The interior minister of Italy forced a car company, Yoyo, to supply cars at a particular price.
9 The police bought cars from Yoyo main dealers.

3 a 2.1 **A lawyer, Andrew, is going on holiday and is handing over some cases to a colleague while he is away. He is discussing one case with another colleague, Janet. Listen and answer these questions.**
1 Who is Andrew's client?
2 What is their business?
3 Who is the client suing?
4 What are their businesses?
5 Why is the client suing them?
6 What has been the reaction of the respondents?

b Complete the gaps in the Elements column of the chart on the opposite page using the words in the box.

> commerce   conspiracy   forbids   illegal   monopoly

c 2.1 **Listen again and correct the information in the Factual propositions column.**

Elements	Factual propositions	Facts
Section 1 of Sherman Act makes (1) _____ any contract, combination or (2) _____ in restraint of trade. Section 2 (3) _____ any person or entity from monopolizing or attempting to monopolize.	TVs 20% and refrigerators 40% over the cost to others.	January 2008: Baker and others told Jupiter they would only sell at 20% and 40% over the cost to others.
Section 1 of Sherman Act prohibits monopolization of interstate (4) _____ which tends to create a (5) _____ .	Very large business, established for many years, but size of business relevant.	Small business open 24 hours a day; Competition Acts do not apply.

4 🎧 **5** **2.2** Listen to the next part of the conversation and complete the facts that Andrew and Janet are going to add to the chart.

1 Baker Retail told Jupiter in _____ that they would sell at 20% over.
2 James Hull phoned them three times in the week of _____ .
3 He called Cool Places _____ times in the week of _____ .
4 The relevant letters about him being a small merchant were dated _____ , _____ and _____ .
5 He contacted them regarding the Zoony range about _____ times.
6 The TV models were _____ .

5 Complete these expressions that Andrew used to check the information.

1 When _____ was that?
2 And when did you _____ … ?
3 Sorry, what was _____ last date?
4 And you mentioned _____ about …
5 _____ you say …?
6 Could you _____ give me that again?

Language work

6 a Complete this dialogue using expressions from the Useful language box.

A: A Mrs Jane Bradley phoned this morning. It was about her brother's case.
B: _____?
A: Jane Bradley.
B: _____?
A: 10.15 this morning.
B: _____?
A: She wanted to know how her brother's case is progressing.

b Work in pairs. Write a similar dialogue for another pair to complete.

USEFUL LANGUAGE

Checking information or asking for clarification

Sorry, I didn't catch that.	Sorry, I'm not following.	And who/where/what/when …
What was that last point?	So … what are you saying?	I'm afraid you've lost me.
What was that name again?	And your point is …?	

Writing

1 Discuss these questions with a partner.
1 How strong do you think Jupiter Electronics's case is?
2 What do you think might happen next?

2 Andrew is writing a memo to Sylvia about the Jupiter case and is going to attach the legal elements chart. Match these descriptions (a–g) with the sections of the memo below (1–7).

a Informing where reader can find additional information
b Outlining writer's situation / reason for writing
c Headings
d Closings
e Specifying subject of memo
f Suggesting (possible) action
g Summarizing main point(s) / information reader needs

1 → TO:
   FROM:

2 → As you know, I …
3 → There are several cases pending that you may have to deal with while I'm away. One of these is …
4 → It concerns …
5 → You may have to …
6 → I'm attaching …
7 → Thank you for all your help.

3 Which memo sections in Exercise 2 (a–g) could these phrases be used in?

1 As promised, …
  As requested, …
  As you know, …
  As expected, …
  You may be aware that …
  Due to the fact that …
  This is to inform you that …

2 The case concerns …
  The main points of the case are as follows: …
  Here is a brief outline of …

3 Please see attached document(s) for further details.
  Please contact … for further details.
  Don't hesitate to contact … for further details.
  … shall / will be available to assist you.

4 I suggest …
  You will / may need to …
  Should … happen, …

4 Use the framework in Exercise 2 to write Andrew's memo to Sylvia.

Speaking

1 a Work in pairs. Read this situation and discuss the task with your partner.

> You and you partner work in a law firm. Your client owns a small cruise liner. He believes that two larger cruise companies are conspiring to fix prices and has asked for your advice. Discuss what advice to give him.
>
> - Problems involved in proving a price-fixing conspiracy
> - What legal action to take
> - Costs involved in taking proceedings or not taking proceedings
> - Alternative action

'Thank heavens I saved my teddy bear – he brings me good luck.'

b Compare your advice with other students in the group.

2 Write a memo to inform your senior partner about the case and the action you have advised. You can use either the points you and your partner discussed or points from the lawyers' conversation.

Language work

3 Make adjectives from the words in the box and put them in the correct columns of the chart below, according to their endings.

| abuse | commerce | compete | crime | discriminate | dominate | economy |
| enforce | favour | finance | influence | predator | restrict | statute | vary |

–ive	–able	–ant	–ial	–al	–ory	–ic

4 a The adjectives in Exercise 3 are all from this unit. Can you remember the context they appeared in? Without looking back, choose five of the adjectives and write a sentence using each, related to competition law.

b Can you add two more adjectives to each column of the table?

Reading: Part 2

1 Read this extract from a website article about competition law and sharing information among companies. Think of the best word to fill each gap.

TIP
Always read the whole sentence before trying to find the word to fill the gap. The word needs to fit the structure *and* the meaning.

Competition law and sharing information among companies

Information exchange between companies is (0) __an__ everyday commercial reality. If companies (1) _____ exchange information, commercial life would grind to an abrupt halt, as nobody would ever be (2) _____ to reach agreement. Even competitors may publish certain information in (3) _____ that those active in the market can gauge the general health of an industry. Without (4) _____ exchanges, important investment decisions by the businesses themselves, as (5) _____ as by investors and government, would be made in the dark. (6) _____ this, companies must be very careful when making information available, as sharing too (7) _____ information could breach competition law and create exposure to the risk of a large fine or even criminal sanctions (8) _____ individuals.

Competition law becomes relevant when the nature of the information exchanged between current or potential competitors (9) _____ it easier for them to predict each others' behaviour and adjust (10) _____ own accordingly. This in its most severe form may ultimately enable participants to fix prices or allocate customers or markets – in other words, create a cartel. The risk is greatest when information passes between current or potential competitors. For this reason, (11) _____ is this exchange of information that is most strictly controlled (and punished) by competition law. Information exchange between supplier and buyer is (12) _____ only permissible but necessary if they are to reach a commercial agreement. Nevertheless, even this information exchange can cause problems where that information could be used to fix the buyer's resale prices for end customers.

Speaking: Part 3

TIP
In this part of the test, you must interact with your partner. Be careful that you talk to each other and not to the examiner.

You run legal training programmes for different companies. One of your clients has asked you to give a day's programme on competition law. Decide what you should include in the programme and why.

Discussion points
- Anti-competitive activity
- Consequences of breach
- How to achieve compliance

2 Competition law

Writing: Part 2

TIP
Make sure that you divide your memo up into different sections. One long paragraph or lots of single sentences are not good ways to present information.

You have invited a training agency to deliver a day's training course for your employees on competition law.
Write a memorandum to your employees to tell them about the event. Your memorandum should:

- explain the reason(s) for organizing the training day
- inform them of the main content of the course
- give details of times
- indicate what action they should take on receiving the memo, including any questions on competition law for the trainers.

Write your answer in 200–250 words.

Listening: Part 1

TIP
Before listening, read the questions or stems carefully so that you know the information you are listening for.

You will hear three different extracts. Choose the answer (A, B or C) which fits best, according to what you hear. There are two questions for each extract.

  2.3 Extract 1
You will hear two lawyers discussing a training programme.

1 The man is not going on the course because …
   A of work pressure.
   B the course is expensive.
   C he has already been on several courses this year.

2 The woman is looking forward to …
   A meeting different people.
   B going to lectures.
   C participating in certain activities.

  2.3 Extract 2
You will hear two lawyers discussing an inquiry by the Office of Fair Trading (OFT).

3 In both lawyers' opinion, the OFT inquiry is …
   A justified.
   B a waste of money.
   C not based on any real evidence.

4 The man believes that the big supermarkets …
   A cheat their customers.
   B often over price their dairy products.
   C need watching.

  2.3 Extract 3
You will hear a lawyer talking to a colleague about his studies in competition law.

5 According to the man, …
   A studying at the Oxford college is preferable to studying in Paris.
   B the Oxford college is the only place to offer certain courses.
   C the Oxford college only runs competition-law programmes.

6 How has the course benefited the man?
   A He now uses English all the time.
   B He has a lot of useful contacts.
   C He has a lot of academic respect.

3 Employment law

■ **Lead-in** | **Discuss these questions with a partner.**
1 What types of situation does a lawyer who specializes in employment law have to advise on?
2 What types of difference do you think there are between employment law in different jurisdictions?
3 How important is it for a lawyer to be aware of international employment law? Why?

Reading 1

1 **Read the first paragraph of the article on employment law on the opposite page and answer these questions.**
   1 Why is international employment law changing?
   2 When and why might a country decide to ratify a convention?
   3 What is the main foundation for a lot of labour law conventions?

2 **Complete the second paragraph of the article using the words in the box.**

| benefits | dismissal | drafting | facility | pension | perspective | race |
| reductions | severance | terminating | transactions | unions | workforce |

3 **Match each of these comments and questions from an employer (1–8) with a practical issue mentioned in the article. Two relate to the same issue.**

1 I'm thinking of letting Mark go, because at his age, the job's getting a bit too much for him.

2 When people retire, I want them to have a decent income.

3 We've got a new project, and I need to take on more staff.

4 How long do we need to continue paying staff when they are off sick?

5 A woman would never be strong enough to do that job. But what do I put in the advert?

6 Business is getting worse. I'm going to have to lose ten men. What do I need to pay them? They've worked for me for five years.

7 This guy is really lazy – I want to fire him. How do I go about it?

8 I presume we need a clause about the number of days annual leave?

Language work

4 a **Which verbs relate to these nouns?**
   1 consolidation   4 discrimination
   2 ratification   5 legislation
   3 termination   6 regulation

   b **One of the verbs has a different ending to the rest. Which one?**

   c **Mark the stress on the nouns and verbs. What do you notice?**

28   3 Employment law

International labour law and employment law

The field of international labour law and employment law is developing rapidly and changing to fit the needs of increasingly global business. While international law applies only between entities that can claim international personality, national law is the internal law of states that regulates the conduct of individuals and other legal entities within their jurisdiction. When the labour legislation or practice of a country has reached a certain level, it may be desirable for the country to ratify a convention that provides for a standard corresponding to the existing national situation. In international labour law, there are many conventions, based on the notion of social justice and designed to create international obligations for the states that ratify them. Ratification of respective conventions can contribute to the consolidation of national labour legislation by acting as a guarantee against backsliding by governments responding to economic conditions.

Lawyers, law students and counsel increasingly recognize the importance of having a global **(1)** _____ on labour and employment law. Corporate lawyers frequently have to deal with a variety of labour and employment problems internationally in structuring corporate **(2)** _____ . They are expected to have a national and an international knowledge of requirements affecting practical issues such as establishing a **(3)** _____ , hiring a **(4)** _____ , **(5)** _____ employment contracts, **(6)** _____ the employment of or replacing employees, providing wages and **(7)** _____ , dealing with **(8)** _____ , carrying out workforce **(9)** _____ , selling the business, and paying **(10)** _____ through redundancy or **(11)** _____ schemes. In addition, issues such as discrimination on grounds of gender, **(12)** _____ or disability may arise in advertising, recruitment and **(13)** _____ processes. Therefore knowledge of international labour law and the national employment law of particular countries is vitally important for counsel specializing in these areas.

Reading 2

1 Answer these questions.

1 What is the difference between an act and a convention?
2 Where do you find an article, and where do you find a section?

2 These are the seven core International Labour Organization Conventions. Discuss what each one concerns with a partner. Do you know how they have been incorporated into your own national legislations?

1 Abolition of Forced Labour Convention
2 Convention Concerning Freedom of Association and Protection of the Right to Organize
3 Discrimination (Employment and Occupation) Convention
4 Equal Remuneration Convention
5 Forced Labour Convention
6 Minimum Age Convention
7 Right to Organize and Collective Bargaining Convention

3 Read these extracts from three of the conventions in Exercise 2. Which conventions are they from?

A

1 Workers' and employers' organizations shall have the right to draw up their constitutions and rules, to elect their representatives in full freedom and to formulate their programmes.
2 The public authorities shall refrain from any interference which would restrict this right or impede the lawful exercise thereof.

B

1 Workers shall enjoy adequate protection against acts of anti-union discrimination in respect of their employment.

2 Such protection shall apply more particularly in respect of acts calculated to:
  a) make the employment of a worker subject to the condition that he shall not join a union or shall relinquish trade union membership;
  b) cause the dismissal of or otherwise prejudice a worker by reason of union membership or because of participation in union activities outside working hours or, with the consent of the employer, within working hours.

C

Notwithstanding the provisions of paragraph 1 of this Article, national laws or regulations or the competent authority may, after consultation with the organizations of employers and workers concerned, where such exist, authorize employment or work as from the age of 16 years on condition that the health, safety and morals of the young persons concerned are fully protected and that the young persons have received adequate specific instruction or vocational training in the relevant branch of activity.

4 Match these expressions (1–12) with their highlighted synonyms in the extracts.

1 of this	5 conditions	9 these
2 agreement	6 stop themselves	10 give up
3 related to	7 despite	11 in any other way
4 because of	8 have the right to	12 allow

5 Read these extracts from other conventions and choose the best options.

> Each member of the International Labour Organization which ratifies this Convention **(1)** *undertakes / promises* to **(2)** *oppose / suppress* the use of forced or compulsory labour in all its forms within the shortest possible period.

> With a **(3)** *sight / view* to this complete suppression, **(4)** *recourse / resort* to forced or compulsory labour may be had, during the transitional period, for public purposes only and as an exceptional **(5)** *measure / action*, subject to the conditions and guarantees **(6)** *hereto / hereinafter* provided.

Listening

1 Discuss these questions with a partner.
1. What procedures are available for dealing with employment disputes?
2. What is 'mediation'?
3. Why is mediation popular?
4. What skills do you think a mediator needs?

'A tea break every four hours, a rest room with TV and air conditioning throughout the meeting, otherwise no agreement.'

3 Employment law

2 🎧 **3.1 Listen to a conversation about being a mediator and decide whether these statements are true or false.**

1 Hannah hasn't met John before.
2 John has been working in employment law for a very long time.
3 John knows a lot about mediating.
4 A mediator should not favour one party.
5 John's client continues to work with her boss.
6 Mediation should take place away from the employee's environment.
7 Parties in a mediation must tell the truth.
8 Mediating is similar to what lawyers do.
9 John admires Hannah's work.

3 🎧 **3.1 Listen again. Who must do these things in a mediation: the mediator (M) or the parties (P)?**

1 Be neutral.
2 Adopt a more positive view.
3 Talk honestly and frankly.
4 Create a safe environment.
5 Move towards improved relationships.
6 Identify needs and interests.
7 Reach a mutually acceptable solution.
8 Reduce tension and anxiety.
9 Be able to read people.
10 Support both parties.

Language work

4 Match the words in the left column (1–8) with the words in the right column (a–h) to make collocations from the conversation.

1 vested   a control
2 follow   b interest
3 self   c the momentum
4 informed   d move
5 mutually   e a career
6 common   f decisions
7 career   g acceptable
8 maintain   h aim

'So we're agreed: we'll go to mediation.'

Speaking 1

1 Explain your job in the legal profession to a partner. If you haven't worked in the legal profession yet, imagine a job you would like to have. You can use the expressions that Hannah used to explain her job as a mediator.

USEFUL LANGUAGE

The important thing about a mediator is …
We must be …
What we do is …
A basic part of our training is …
This means we can …
The mediator's job is to …
You really have to be able to …

2 a Complete the stages in a mediation (1–12) using the words in the box.

| agreement | allow | ask for | build | effect | explain | hear |
| identify | name | positions | probe | trade-offs |

1 _____ parties' stories
2 _____ venting
3 Begin to _____ trust
4 Write an _____
5 Discuss _____ of not resolving
6 _____ the process
7 _____ understanding
8 Focus on interests and _____ of parties
9 _____ areas of agreement
10 _____ desired outcomes
11 Discuss priorities and _____
12 _____ positives

b Complete this table with the above stages. Some stages may go in more than one session.

introduction	first joint session	private sessions	final joint session

3 In groups of three, role-play the introductory session of a mediation.

A You are working on a major project for a construction company. You feel that one of your team members is not pulling his weight. At a meeting last week, you thought the report he prepared was sub-standard and you made a comment about the quality of the work. He became defensive and the subject was dropped, although there is still tension between you both, which is affecting the work. You are angry with him, but feel that the subject should have been handled differently. You are going to mediation to resolve the matter because you feel that the situation might grow worse.

B Your boss gave you a dressing-down because there were some errors in a major report you worked on that just went out. You were very angry because you had worked very hard and long hours to finish the report. You could have fixed most of the problems if your boss hadn't made so many last-minute changes. After your boss finished her outburst, you said 'You're impossible! I'm not going to deal with this!' and you left the room. You have come to mediation to vent and to figure out what to do.

C You are the mediator. Here is some useful language for you.

First, we're going to …
Then, we'll be …
So, to begin with …
Now, I'd like you to …
What do you expect from … ?

3 Employment law

Writing

1 Read the letter below from a client, Mr Bennett, to his lawyer, Miss James. In what order should these points be in her letter?

a summary of mediation process ❏
b recommendation of a mediator ❏
c offer to mediate yourself ❏
d your opinions ❏
e advice on dealing with the problem ❏
f reference to Mr Bennett's letter ❏
g attachment with further details ❏

> Norwood
> NP25 6TT
> 4th February
>
> Dear Miss James,
>
> A difficult situation has arisen at work involving two of my key employees, and I am considering bringing in a mediator. Do you think this is a good idea?
> I am not completely sure what mediation involves. Perhaps you could give me a brief outline and also the name of someone I can contact.
>
> Yours sincerely
> Jake Bennett

2 For each of these phrases, indicate whether they would be used to refer to previous letter (RF), give an opinion (O), summarize (S), recommend (RC) or attach (A).

1 Depending on the situation, this can be a good idea.
2 Please see the attached document for further details on …
3 Mediation can be a good way forward because …
4 In the past, I have recommended …
5 It is my opinion that …
6 In response to your query regarding …
7 Briefly, the process begins with …
8 This process can be of benefit to all parties.
9 I would recommend a colleague of mine.
10 With reference to your letter of 8th October, …
11 I think you should look into the matter further.
12 I attach a document that goes into more detail about the benefits of mediation.

3 Write the letter from Miss James to Mr Bennett. Follow these steps.

1 Make notes and divide them into paragraphs.
2 Write a draft letter.
3 Check for mistakes.
4 Exchange your letter with a partner and check each other's work.
5 Write the final draft.

4 Read these five extracts from letters a lawyer has received from different clients concerning employment issues. Work in pairs. First, discuss the issues, then write a short paragraph dealing with each one. Do not write complete letters.

1 I do not think that my employer is complying with health and safety rules in the workplace. What should I do?

2 I have recently been dismissed by my employer for selling trade secrets to a rival company. This is completely untrue!

3 Could you please send me some recent case studies on unfair dismissal? Thanks.

4 When employing new staff, what should I be careful about concerning discrimination?

5 I would like to hold a workshop for my employees on employment law and their rights. Do you think this is a good thing, and can you recommend a training company?

Speaking 2

Work in pairs. You are going to talk for about a minute on one of the topics below. Each topic is accompanied by some words that you may wish to use.

- Before you start your talk, check that you understand all the vocabulary and, if necessary, do some research on the topic.
- After your partner's talk, ask at least one question about what he/she has said.
- Write a short summary of your partner's talk. Remember to:
  – mention the main points
  – give the most important information
  – use your own words.

USEFUL LANGUAGE

My partner talked about …
He/She began by saying that …
He/She believes that …
He/She considers …
According to my partner, …
The most important point he/she mentioned was …
He/She finished by concluding that …

A Disciplining employees

- Importance of having clear procedures
- What these are/might be
- Difference between 'capability' issues and punishable actions
- What constitutes 'misconduct'

- allegation of misconduct • appropriate
- ascertain the facts
- convene a disciplinary hearing
- disciplinary • internal disciplinary procedure
- malingering • proportionate to
- right to appeal • sanction
- statutory procedures • underperforming
- witnesses

B Unfair dismissal

- What constitutes 'unfair dismissal'
- Advantages and disadvantages of employment tribunal over arbitration
- The system in your country

- allegations • confidentiality
- defamation of character • discrimination
- evidence • follow procedure
- gross misconduct • legal representation
- length of service • record • redundancy
- trade unions

Reading: Part 5

TIP
There are often references in either the sentences or the main text to something that has come before or that will follow. Check for words like *this*, *that*, *it*, *they*, *he*, etc.

Read this extract from a legal article and choose the best sentence (A–H) to fill each of the gaps. There is one extra sentence which you do not need to use.

Resolving employment disputes through mediation

National procedures available for the resolution of employment disputes range from taking proceedings through the courts to having the disputes heard by employment tribunals. **(1)** _____ The adverse publicity can cause devastation for a well-established business, the distraction of an otherwise strong and efficient management team and a psychological effect on the business at hand. Once litigation has begun, it is often very difficult to stop. **(2)** _____ Frequently, companies find themselves resolving cases on the steps of the court after considerable economic, political and emotional cost.

(3) _____ An existing employee may contend that supervisory personnel have harassed them. A person whose employment has been terminated or who has been denied promotion may contend that such action constitutes discrimination based on race, colour, sex, national origin, age or disability. **(4)** _____ National laws, with the influence and assistance of international conventions, reflect social intolerance for certain workplace conduct, and court decisions are redefining the manner in which an employer must relate to its employees. **(5)** _____ They are often unique because the perceptions of men and women may differ as to what is appropriate conduct. **(6)** _____ When an employee's employment has been terminated or when a current employee makes a claim against his/her employer, it is generally in the interests of both parties to attempt to resolve the matter early through a procedure called 'mediation'. Mediation is especially effective in dealing with a myriad of legal, factual and emotional issues that are frequently present in a dispute. **(7)** _____

A Because of this, employment disputes based on gender perceptions can be more difficult to resolve.
B Each step of the process leads to the next.
C All employees need to be aware of the complications that may develop from using alternative methods.
D It can also provide a cost-effective and mutually satisfying way of negotiating what are otherwise difficult disputes.
E Disputes between a company and its employees can arise in difficult situations.
F However, one of the most damaging controversies for a business is a dispute with an employee.
G Employment disputes grow out of relationships.
H He or she may believe that their employment has been wrongfully terminated and that the termination was unfair or without good cause.

Speaking: Part 3

TIP
If you don't know what to say about one of the discussion points, don't worry. They are given to help you – you don't have to talk about all of them.

One of your clients has just started a new business. He wants your advice on what to consider when hiring staff.

Discussion points
- Avoiding discrimination in advertising
- Checking authenticity of references and CVs
- What to include in contracts

3 Employment law

Writing: Part 1

TIP
You must make some reference to all the notes made on the letter or you will automatically lose marks.

Your are a lawyer, and one of your clients, Carl Posner, has just started his own business. Mr Posner has written to you asking for some advice on disciplinary matters. Read his letter, on which you have made some notes. Then, using all the information in your notes, write a reply to Mr Posner.

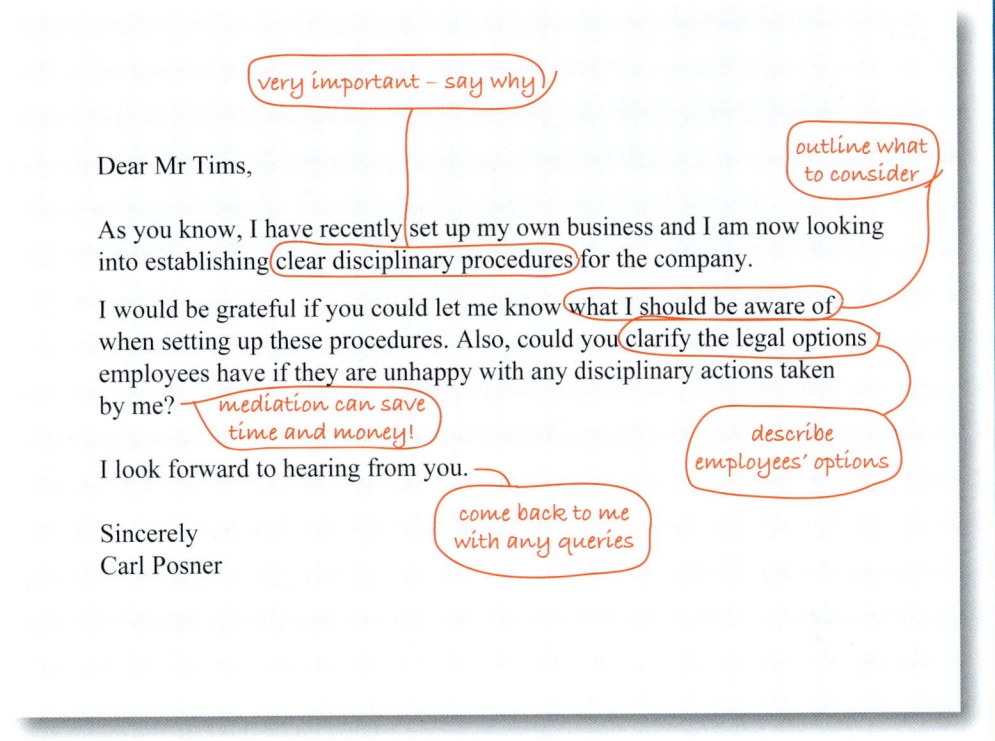

Dear Mr Tims,

As you know, I have recently set up my own business and I am now looking into establishing clear disciplinary procedures for the company. *— very important – say why*

I would be grateful if you could let me know what I should be aware of when setting up these procedures. *— outline what to consider* Also, could you clarify the legal options employees have if they are unhappy with any disciplinary actions taken by me? *— describe employees' options* *mediation can save time and money!*

I look forward to hearing from you. *— come back to me with any queries*

Sincerely
Carl Posner

Listening: Part 2

TIP
Remember that two of the three choices will be distracters. There will be some reference to them in the listening, but they will not actually answer the question. Don't choose an answer simply because you hear a specific word. Make sure it fits the meaning.

🎧 10 **3.2** You will hear part of a conversation between a lawyer and her client about misuse of communications systems at work. For each question, choose the best answer: a, b or c.

1 The client is mainly worried about …
   a a particular member of his staff.
   b protecting the security of his computer systems.
   c his staff's use of the internet.

2 The lawyer points out that …
   a employees spend a lot of time on social networking sites.
   b employers can be considered responsible for their employees' misuse of the internet.
   c employees can be prosecuted for writing bad things about their employers in emails.

3 The client wants advice on …
   a how he can legally film his employees at work.
   b the laws of privacy.
   c the options available to him.

4 In the lawyer's opinion, …
   a her client shouldn't create a bad relationship with his staff.
   b her client needs to protect his own privacy.
   c employees have greater rights than employers in this situation.

5 The lawyer suggests …
   a printing off a policy from the internet.
   b monitoring as a last course of action.
   c taking disciplinary measures against those who don't comply.

3 Employment law

4 Contract law 1

■ **Lead-in** Discuss this question with a partner.

Have you ever drafted or helped draft a contract?

If yes, what were the difficulties or problems?

If no, what do you think the difficulties or problems might be?

Reading 1

1 a Answer these questions.
1. What general advice would you give someone who is drafting a contract?
2. What effects can legal disputes over contracts have on a company?
3. What should be included in an international contract?

b Read the first part of a guide to drafting commercial contracts on the opposite page to check your answers.

2 Read the second part of the guide and answer these questions.
1. Why should contract negotiating be done before the drafting stage?
2. What is the *contra preferendum* rule?
3. What is a basic rule for expressing the same idea more than once in a contract?
4. Why is it a good thing to use standard clauses when drafting a contract?
5. Find two examples of typical mistakes.
6. What are the three most important sets of universal rules on contracts?

Language work

3 Write the adjective related to each of these nouns. Underline the stressed syllable of each adjective.

1. ambiguity
2. availability
3. confidentiality
4. liability
5. advisability
6. typicality

4 Some words from the text are often confused with others. Use a dictionary to find the differences between these pairs of words or phrases.

1. warranty / guarantee
2. set / group
3. terms / clause
4. duty / right
5. termination / finalization
6. comprise / include
7. remedies / arbitration
8. construed / believed
9. numerous / a number of

5 Complete these sentences using the correct words from Exercise 4.

1. The _____ on my car runs out in two months.
2. What _____ are available to the injured party in case of breach of contract?
3. The public has a _____ to report any wrongdoing to the authorities.
4. _____ of an employee's contract of employment can lead to legal action.
5. _____ people have applied for the position and will be interviewed soon.

Drafting a commercial contract

The general advice when drafting a commercial contract is to draft a written contract that is as complete and as precise as possible. The reasons for this are twofold: firstly, there is clear proof of the written terms; and secondly, it reduces the risk of legal disputes. Disputes may be lost in court. They can also be expensive, time consuming and detrimental to the reputation of a company.

A typical structure of an international commercial contract would comprise the following:
- a heading setting out the type of contract
- the names and addresses of the parties
- a description of the goods to be delivered or services to be provided, including quality, quantity, time, etc.
- fixation of price and details of payment
- duties and rights of the parties, e.g. warranty, payment of tax/duty, etc.
- limitation of liability
- remedies in case of breach of duties
- a confidentiality clause
- the duration/termination of the contract
- a force majeure clause setting out circumstances excusing non-fulfilment in case of natural disasters, war, etc.
- a clause on the governing law of the contract
- an arbitration clause
- signatures of the parties and date of signing
- appendices containing definitions, timetables, etc.

Points to remember

1. For the terms to be clear, the process of drafting is not the time to negotiate matters of principle. This should be done before drafting commences.
2. Clarity and certainty of expression are very important, as any ambiguity of expression is often construed by a court against the person who is trying to rely on it, particularly if he is the person who has drafted the clause. This is known as the *contra preferendum* rule.
3. Never express the same idea in two different ways in the contract; it is always better to repeat the same sentence. For example, do not use the sentence 'to the best of the vendor's knowledge and belief' in one place and 'to the best of the vendor's belief' in another. Typical sources of mistakes in commercial contracts can be as basic as different date formats (for example 3/4/2010 may be interpreted as 3rd April 2010 or 4th March 2010) or when mentioning currencies (for example, $ may be USD or AUD).
4. The use of standard clauses wherever possible is important, as such clauses are familiar to both sides and save valuable time, and are likely to cover the important points. However, never draft in isolation, and make sure that the standard clauses actually cover what is intended by the parties.
5. Also be aware of the law which can affect the contract. There are numerous sets of universal rules on contracts covering different aspects of international commerce and created by different institutions. The most important of these are the rules under the UN Convention on Contracts for the International Sale of Goods 1980 (CISG), the UNIDROIT Principles of International Commercial Contracts 2004 and the ICC Incoterms 2000. The application of these rules depends on several factors: the set of rules in question, whether their application is automatic or determined by the parties' agreement on their application, and whether these rules are available in all states.

Reading 2

1 **Discuss these questions with a partner.**
 1 What is necessary to make a contract enforceable?
 2 Does a contract always need to be written?

2 **Read the article below, then discuss these questions in groups.**
 1 What are the features of an 'exchange relationship'?
 2 What is the significance of 'assent'?
 3 How do courts determine agreement?
 4 What is the difference between CISG and UNIDROIT?

Enforceability of contracts

The essential feature of a contractual relationship is that it is an exchange relationship which is voluntary and consensual. It can be created by oral or written agreement between two or more parties. It contains at least one promise and is recognized in law as enforceable. The element of agreement distinguishes contractual obligations from many other kinds of legal duty that arise by operation of law from some act or event where there is no necessity for assent. By entering into an agreement, the parties bind themselves to each other for the common purpose of the contract, and therefore the essence of the contract is the relationship. To determine whether the parties actually agreed to the contract and whether they agreed to all the terms of the contract is not always easy. In deciding whether a person actually agreed to a contract, the law usually looks objectively at the intent of the parties.

Oral contracts may be enforceable in certain circumstances, whereas certain types of contracts must be recorded in writing and signed in order to be enforceable. The legal doctrine known as the *statute of frauds* was developed in English common law, but similar rules have been codified in other jurisdictions, including the United States.

For contract formation, certain requirements are necessary to ensure valid enforceable contracts under common and civil law. However, in order to remove ambiguities caused by different domestic laws concerning contracts for the international sales of goods, the United Nations Convention on Contracts for the International Sale of Goods (CISG) was adopted in 1980. Unless specifically excluded, it applies to contracts between companies located in different countries and, to date, over two-thirds of the world's countries have ratified this Convention. While the CISG provides a uniformed text of laws for international sales of goods, the UNIDROIT Principles are a non-binding attempt to reach a progressive harmonization of the general principles of contract law. The aim of UNIDROIT is to establish a balanced set of rules designed for use throughout the world, irrespective of the legal traditions and the economic and political conditions of the countries in which they are applied.

Language work

3 Find synonyms for these words in the article.

1 very important
2 without outside pressure
3 agreed by both parties
4 makes it different from
5 tie
6 the same for each
7 decide
8 legally acceptable
9 officially accepted
10 the same for everyone
11 outside / not concerning

4 Work in pairs. Dictate the words to your partner to test spelling.

5 Do you think UNIDROIT can succeed? Why (not)?

Listening

1 You are going to hear part of a lecture about contract drafting. Before you listen, discuss these questions with a partner.

1 What must a contract establish?
2 What must you plan ahead for?
3 What do you think are the purposes of these clauses?
   a the integration clause
   b the waiver clause
   c the time of the essence clause
   d the survival clause
   e the severability clause

2 🎧 4.1 Listen to the first part of the lecture to check your answers. Then match these explanations with the clauses in question 3 of Exercise 1.

1 This clause says that there are no agreements outside the contract.
2 These clauses enable parts of a contract to function without another.
3 This clause enables the continuation of certain agreements after the end date of a contract.

'Sign here to indicate you have no idea what you've signed for.'

3 🎧 12 **4.2** The second part of the lecture is about language in contracts. Listen and complete these guidelines from the handout.

> ## Keeping language simple!
> - Avoid legal (1) _____ and phrases, e.g. *at or* (2) _____, basic and (3) _____, full and (4) _____.
> - Use clear and straightforward verbs wherever possible:
>
> | Complex verbs | Clear alternatives |
> | --- | --- |
> | (5) _____ | do |
> | (6) _____ | make/give/give back |
> | (7) _____ | begin/start |
> | (8) _____ | end/stop |
>
> - Use (9) _____ sentences rather than passive ones.
> - Keep sentences (10) _____.
> - Keep subjects and (11) _____ together.
> - Keep (12) _____ verbs together.

4 According to the guidelines in Exercise 3, how could these sentences be improved?
1 The misrepresentation rendered the contract unenforceable.
2 The chairman commenced the proceedings by reading the agenda.
3 The client's relationship with his lawyers was discontinued immediately.
4 The firm of lawyers with many highly qualified partners and extensive premises including confidential meeting rooms and other facilities for clients was established in 1960.
5 The rent must be promptly paid by the tenant.

Language work

5 Work in pairs. Using a dictionary if necessary, find a simple equivalent to each of these verbs.
1 attempt
2 ascertain
3 forward
4 retain
5 deem
6 inform
7 obtain
8 notify
9 utilize

6 a Choose a reading text from another unit you have studied in this book. Find five verbs and five adjectives that have more simple equivalents.

b Test your partner by giving him/her either the original words or the simpler equivalents to elicit the synonyms.

7 🎧 **13** **4.3** The final part of the lecture is about the process of drafting. Listen and choose the best answers.

1 The first draft should …
   a include all the correct details.
   b be the first of many.
   c be an outline.

2 Concentrating on various clauses can …
   a sometimes cause problems for the whole contract.
   b help avoid ambiguity.
   c fix important problems.

3 Revising should be done …
   a while you are writing.
   b slowly.
   c at the end of the process.

8 Match these words and phrases from the whole lecture (1–7) with their definitions (a–g).

1 establish   a consider something and act
2 address   b rule against
3 self-explanatory   c making perfect
4 contradict   d not needing clarification
5 polishing   e accept that
6 strike down   f create
7 reconcile   g go against

Writing 1

Write a report on the professor's talk. Use some of the verbs from the Useful language box and these points.

1 What a contract must establish
2 Different clauses that are important when drafting contracts
3 Importance of language when drafting
4 The process of drafting and revising

> **USEFUL LANGUAGE**
>
> When you report what someone else has said, you don't have to use *He said that* … all the time. You can use other verbs to make your language more varied and interesting. For example:
>
> • state   • maintain   • explain   • insist   • advise   • suggest
> • remind   • emphasize   • warn
>
> Some of these verbs can be followed by an indirect object, either with or without *to* (e.g. *He advised me that …, He explained to me that …*) and others do not require an indirect object (*She maintained that …, She insisted that …*). One of them (*remind*) must always have an indirect object. Check in a dictionary if you are not sure.

4 Contract law 1

Speaking

1 Imagine you are going to give a short presentation on negotiating contracts. In pairs, think of some points that are important to remember when negotiating.

2 a Read the tips below (1–12). Did you note down any of these? In pairs, talk about what you think they mean.

b Match the tips (1–12) with the explanations and reasons (a–l).

1 Wait after each offer.
2 Get it in writing.
3 Have a fall-back plan.
4 Know your bottom line.
5 Prepare carefully.
6 Determine the extent of the other side's authority.
7 Listen to the other side.
8 Make sure you and the parties understand the contract.
9 Discuss everything, however difficult.
10 Don't be afraid to ask.
11 Know what you want.
12 Avoid using form contracts.

a Negotiators often fail to **raise an issue** because they don't think they will have a chance of success. Don't be shy!

b Make sure you know exactly what you do and do not want. You need to make sure that you do not **end up** with something less than acceptable.

c Never negotiate against yourself. Once you have made an offer, wait for a response before making another offer. If you don't wait, you encourage the other party to **hold off** its response in the hopes of getting an even better offer.

d When parties fail to **live up to** an agreement, written proof of the negotiator's intent is **critical** and helps those resolving the dispute to know what was intended.

e The three most important things about a negotiation are preparation, preparation and preparation. You should **research** the needs and wants of your client and of the other party. You should also be able to **anticipate** different responses and be prepared for how you will react.

f Make sure you know if you are negotiating with the deal-maker or not. If not, you have to convince the party to agree with your position and make sure they understand it so that they can convince someone else.

g By knowing what you want and what you need, you will know when it is time to stop. If you look for more than you need, you may end up losing everything.

h Always keep your best alternative in mind if you are facing an unsuccessful negotiation. If you don't have a fall-back position, you will have to keep negotiating until a deal is reached, even if that agreement is unacceptable.

i Good negotiators are good listeners and good communicators, not only good speakers. By listening, observing behaviour and body language, and **being attentive**, you can learn things that will further your interests.

j Most people don't like to argue. Negotiations should not be arguments, but remember that avoiding **tough** issues may cause problems later on.

k Form contracts merely **drive** negotiations **towards** a predetermined result proposed by one side. The draft contract must reflect the negotiation 100%.

l Never sign anything on behalf of a client or advise a client to sign unless they have fully understood all the contract terms.

Language work

3 Find words and expressions in bold in the explanations in Exercise 2 that mean the following.

1 very important
2 finish
3 predict what is going to happen
4 do what is promised
5 find out about
6 push towards
7 paying attention
8 delay
9 talk about something important
10 hard

4 Rank your top five tips. Compare with other pairs.

Writing 2

You are mentoring a new employee of your law firm. He has asked you for some advice on negotiating successfully. Email the employee giving him some useful advice. Use the phrases in the Useful language box.

> **USEFUL LANGUAGE**
> **Advice and sequencing**
> Most importantly, …
> It's vital that …
> You should always/never …
> In addition to this, …
> It's not a good idea to …
> You must first …
> Following that, …
> My main advice would be to …
> Don't forget to …
> Don't be put off by …
> Always consider …

'Don't let it throw you – it's just a negotiating tactic.'

Reading: Part 2

EXAM PRACTICE

TIP
Look at the words that come before and after the gap to see what sort of word you need. Remember your answer must be correct grammatically, but the sentence/paragraph must also make sense!

Read this extract from a webpage about contract terms. Think of the best word to fill each gap.

Buyers' terms and conditions and unfair contract terms

The Unfair Contract Terms Act

Transactions between businesses are covered **(1)**_____ the Unfair Contract Terms Act 1977 (UCTA). In general, businesses are assumed to be free to enter into **(2)**_____ contracts they agree between themselves – so you should make **(3)**_____ you're happy with the contracts you agree with other businesses. However, UCTA places a number of restrictions on the contract terms businesses can agree to. Specifically, **(4)**_____ lays down rules for the ways in **(5)**_____ vendor businesses can use exclusion clauses to limit liability in certain areas:

- excluding liability for death or injury is not permitted in **(6)**_____ circumstances;
- excluding liability for losses **(7)**_____ by negligence is permitted only if it is reasonable;
- excluding liability for defective or poor-quality goods is also permitted only if it is reasonable.

The test of reasonableness

UCTA doesn't define precisely **(8)**_____ is meant by 'reasonable', but courts will usually take into account:

- the information available to both parties when the contract was drawn **(9)**_____ ;
- whether the contract was negotiated **(10)**_____ is in a standard form;
- whether the purchaser had the bargaining power to negotiate better terms.

Businesses don't have the same protection as individual consumers. A consumer contract excluding liability for defective goods **(11)**_____ be automatically invalid. But as a business purchaser, it's up to you to check in advance what terms and conditions you're agreeing to.

At present, there are separate rules dealing with unfair consumer contracts – the Unfair Terms in Consumer Contracts Regulations.

Sole traders are regarded as businesses **(12)**_____ than consumers for any purchases they make in connection with their business activities. However, if the trader offers you credit terms up to £25,000, you receive the same protection as individuals under the Consumer Credit Act 1974 for this element of the contract.

Speaking: Part 2

TIP
A minute is quite a short time, so don't try to say everything you know about the subject! It's important to try to link the different things you talk about, so make sure you use linking devices to help the listener follow your ideas.

Look at these two topics. Select one of them and give a short talk on it for about a minute. There are some ideas to help you. You have a minute to prepare your talk. After you have finished your talk, your partner will ask you a brief question about it.

TASK 1

Drafting contracts
- What to include
- The importance of using clear English
- The disadvantages of drafting a contract without legal help

TASK 2

Negotiating
- The skills necessary to be a good negotiator
- The importance of preparation
- Knowing when to stop negotiations

4 Contract law 1

Listening: Part 4

🎧 **14–18** **4.4** You will hear five short extracts in which various people talk about the importance of language when drafting contracts. You will need to play each extract twice.

TIP
Don't try to complete both tasks after one listening unless you are very sure of the answers, as you may get confused and miss the next section. Read the questions and possible answers carefully before the first listening and make sure you understand what you're listening for.

TASK ONE

For questions 1–5, choose from the list A–F who is speaking.

A a law student

B a judge

C a senior partner

D a trainer

E a client

F a new lawyer

1 _____   2 _____   3 _____   4 _____   5 _____

TASK TWO

For questions 6–10, choose from the list A–F what the speakers are talking about with regard to drafting contracts.

A old-fashioned language

B a common misconception

C a confusion in terminology

D a proper use of lawyer's skills

E a compromise

F inadequate training

6 _____   7 _____   8 _____   9 _____   10 _____

Writing: Part 2

TIP
When writing the memo, you can use your imagination regarding details about the case as long as you include all the points given. Divide your memo clearly into different sections.

You are moving to a different department in your law firm and you are transferring your remaining cases to a colleague. A client wants to sell electronic equipment to a company in another country. You have been negotiating the contract.

**Write a memorandum to your colleague to brief him on the case.
Your memorandum should:**

- give some information on the client and the deal
- explain what point you have reached in the negotiations
- describe any problems you envisage
- outline what needs to be done next.

Write your answer in 200–250 words.

5 Contract law 2

■ **Lead-in**

Discuss these questions with a partner.
1 What is a breach of contract?
2 What types of breach are there?
3 What can the injured party do when there is a breach of contract?

Reading 1

1 **Read the extract below to check your ideas in the Lead-in.**

2 **Read the extract again and answer these questions.**
1 What two examples of a breach are given?
2 What is the difference between a fundamental and anticipatory breach?
3 What two choices for the innocent party are given in the extract?

Breach of contract

There is a breach of contract when a party to a contract fails to perform his obligations under the contract. Examples of such breach are the failure to supply goods or perform a service as agreed. There are varying degrees of breach, depending on the terms of the contract and the importance of the terms to the core of the contract. A breach of contract does not automatically serve to discharge the contract. Each situation depends on the nature of the breach, but a breach of contract does give the innocent party a number of options to terminate the contract.

The breaches that give rise to such options are **express** or **implied repudiation**, where one party can repudiate the contract as a result of the party in breach failing to perform some terms of the contract. Repudiation before performance is due is known as **anticipatory breach**, where the contract is repudiated before performance is due. **Fundamental breach** is where the party in breach has committed a serious breach of a fundamental term or totally fails to perform the contract. The effect of a repudiatory breach is not always the ending of the contractual relationship. The innocent party does have a couple of choices: he may treat the contract **as discharged by frustration** and bring an action for damages for breach, or he may elect to treat the contract as valid, complete his side of the bargain and then sue for damages from the other party.

3 Use words from the extract to complete these case excerpts.

1 If A has contracted to sell a house to B, and A subsequently sells the same house to C, then this is a(n) _____ of A's obligation to B.

2 If A contracts to sell a house to B, and A subsequently contracts to sell the same house to C and communicates to B that he will not convey the house to B as per the agreement, then A has _____ the agreement with B.

3 If A hires B to start work on 1st June, and A repudiates the contract on 11th May, B is permitted legally to sue on 23rd May, even before the due date of performance of 1st June, as he can sue because of _____ .

4 If A breaches a term of a contract that is so important that it goes to the root of the contract, then the injured party B may terminate the contract and sue for damages for _____ .

5 If A charters a ship to load a cargo for B, and the ship is unfit to sail before the cargo is loaded, so the charterparty cannot be performed, then the contract is discharged by _____ .

4 Work in pairs. Write another case excerpt for each of the different types of breach. Exchange with another pair and guess the types of breach.

Language work

5 Find words or phrases in the extract and excerpts in Exercise 3 that mean the same as the following.

1 result in
2 end
3 choose
4 injured
5 fulfil
6 allow/cause
7 consider
8 basic
9 still legal
10 after this
11 sell
12 employs

6 Complete the table. Which two words remain the same?

verb	noun
perform	(1) _____
supply	(2) _____
discharge	(3) _____
terminate	(4) _____
repudiate	(5) _____
treat	(6) _____
fail	(7) _____
imply	(8) _____

7 Use words from the table in Exercise 6 to complete these sentences.

1 We went ahead because of the _____ that the offer might be withdrawn.

2 His _____ to win support from his colleagues resulted in the company dropping the case.

3 The _____ of all information must be completely confidential.

4 The delay in the _____ of oil caused serious problems.

5 The other party was making outrageous demands, and the _____ of negotiations was the only alternative.

5 Contract law 2

Reading 2

1 Discuss these questions with a partner.
1 Have you ever dealt with an e-contract?
2 List what you think are the main problems with e-contracts.

2 a Work in pairs. Read through these questions about e-contracts. How many can you answer?
1 Why is it very important to read the terms and conditions of a contractual transaction online very carefully before clicking 'I agree'?
2 What are the different types of e-contracts?
3 What specific problems can businesses have concerning e-contracts?
4 What global standard is there to harmonize regulations concerning e-commerce contracts?
5 Why is e-commerce important for developing countries?
6 What do courts consider in disputes over validity of e-contracts?
7 What other developments are happening in the field of e-commerce control?

b Read this extract and find the answers to the questions.

Online contractual transactions are becoming increasingly common, and it is essential that those entering such transactions examine the terms and conditions carefully before clicking on 'I agree' to indicate acceptance, as courts are inclined to uphold agreements accepted in this way.

There are two main types of e-contracts: B2C contracts between businesses and consumers, and B2B contracts, which are between businesses and businesses. Obviously, there are jurisdictional issues that arise because of the global scope of the Internet, and agreements affect the jurisdiction and specify laws that will govern the transactions. Technology also brings with it other risks for companies. Data protection and privacy issues must be dealt with by companies to limit their exposure to liability.

The need to regulate requirements concerning e-commerce contracts led to the setting up of UNCITRAL Model Law on Electronic Commerce in 1996 to set general conditions. It confirms that clicking 'I agree' on a website constitutes a valid form of consent and allows an offer to be made and accepted in electronic form. UNCITRAL Mode Laws have been enacted nationally worldwide and are also important for developing countries, as e-commerce greatly facilitates and protects new businesses in accessing new markets.

However, as with paper-based contracts, electronic contracts are not automatically valid, and in disputes, courts consider whether the parties involved were fully aware of the terms. This sometimes involves deciding how clear the terms were in relation to the size of text or location on a website.

Developments in the law governing e-commerce are continuing. Recently, we have seen a Model Law on Electronic Signatures, which has already been adopted by the national law of certain countries. Other developments currently being considered include an international treaty on Jurisdiction and the Enforcement of Judgements and a global agreement on e-commerce taxation regulations.

3 Discuss this question in small groups.
What legal steps do you think will be taken in the future regarding e-contracts? Why?

Reading 3

1 Discuss these questions with a partner.
1. What does CISG stand for?
2. When might a contract be avoided?
3. What is *foreseeability*?
4. Why might the guidance about what constitutes a fundamental breach be vague under CISG?

2 Read these comments that three student lawyers made following a lecture on aspects of contractual breach. Match the speakers (1–3) with the statements (a–g).

1 The lecture was a bit complicated but … but I think I got the main idea. Where there is a breach of contract, there are a lot of different sorts of remedies available to the innocent party. The types of remedies may vary, depending on the type of breach and also the applicable law. For instance, the CISG – you know, the UN Convention on Contracts for the International Sale of Goods – says that if there is a fundamental breach, then the contract may be avoided. In other words, the breach is so serious that the other party can't get what he expected under the contract. What's important is that if the party in breach or a reasonable person of the same kind and in the same circumstances could've foreseen the damage to the other party, then the breach is fundamental.

2 Yes. It's all about foreseeability, isn't it? We have to look into the future and work out what might be the most likely result, then work backwards. It appears that foreseeability of a loss affects both fundamental breach and non-fundamental breach. If the loss or damage to the affected party – or, as our lecturer put it, detriment – was not foreseeable and it can be proved, then lack of foreseeability is a ground for excuse. However, the burden of proving forseeability rests with the breaching party. So, in a nutshell, if what happened couldn't've been predicted, and the breaching party can prove this, then there is no fundamental breach, right?

3 I think so. I can understand that the type of breach seems to determine the damages that can be looked for. But it's difficult to get clear guidance on what actually constitutes a fundamental breach – which is really pretty fundamental, wouldn't you say?! The lecturer suggested that the vagueness in Article 25 of the CISG is because of the differences which exist across all the definitions of fundamental breach in the various legal systems. This seems to be the reason why the drafters couldn't agree on the type of breach that leads to avoidance of the contract. All the convention does really is provide interpretative guidelines, which surely leaves lawyers a bit in the dark, don't you think?

a Lawyers often have to use prediction in their work.
b It's up to the breaching party to show that no damage was forseeable.
c A breach is fundamental if a reasonable person could have predicted the damage.
d Lawyers have to weigh up what might constitute a fundamental breach.
e The CISG isn't clear about this point because different legal systems interpret fundamental breach differently.
f Loss forseeability does not only affect fundamental breach.
g Remedy options depend on the type of breach.

Language work

3 Match the expressions in *italics* (1–6) to their more formal meanings (a–f).

1 I think I got *the main idea*.
2 *In other words*, …
3 *It's all about* …
4 So, *in a nutshell*, …
5 It's really pretty fundamental, *wouldn't you say*?
6 It surely leaves lawyers a bit *in the dark*, don't you think?

a not knowing what is happening
b most important point
c to summarize
d to express it in a different way
e I'm sure you agree
f it mainly concerns

Listening

1 a How many different types of damages can you name?

b 🎧 5.1 Look at the table and read the definitions. Listen and complete the left-hand column.

Type of damages	When applicable
(1) _____	When the amount of damages is fixed
(2) _____	
(3) _____	When damages have to be vouched
(4) _____	When compensation is given because of loss experienced through relying on the contract
(5) _____	When damages relate to the type of breach and do not have to be vouched like special damages
(6) _____	When the court orders a party to complete the contract

2 🎧 5.1 Listen again. Who says the following: Pavla (P) or Stefan (S)?

1 Could you go through it with me?
2 I get you.
3 You bet!
4 Got that.
5 It's quite straightforward.
6 Is that it?
7 No problem.
8 Sounds a bit confusing.
9 OK so far?
10 Nearly there.
11 You've lost me.
12 And equity is …?

Speaking

1 Work in pairs. Look at the transcript for audio 5.1 on page 100. Practise reading the dialogue. Take the different parts in turn.

2 Work in pairs.

Student A: Imagine you have missed a lesson or lecture about one of the themes from this unit – types of breach, aspects of breach, e-contracts or remedies (or one of the previous units in the book).

Student B: You attended the lesson and have your notes. Role-play the conversation, using expressions from Listening, Exercise 2.

Writing

1 a You're going to read a memo asking for advice about a case. Check you understand the meanings of these words.

| conformity   defective   handy   loss   rubber   selling point   waterproof |

b Read the memo on the opposite page and complete the gaps using the words in the box above.

52   5 Contract law 2

Hi Harry,

Conrad tells me that you recently went to an international conference on 'The Economic (1)_____ Approach to the Connection between (2)_____ Goods and Fundamental Breach'. I hope it was good; I'm really sorry that I missed it, as it would have come in (3)_____ right now.

I have a situation and I think you may be able to help me out. I have a client who contracted to buy 100,000 (4)_____ boots made from natural (5)_____, sourced in Vietnam. Apparently, the big (6)_____ was that the rubber came from Vietnam, and Vietnamese rubber is apparently the best! However, he's found out that although the boots were made in Vietnam, they used rubber sourced in China. He is now left with 100,000 pairs of boots that he says he can't sell because the certificate of (7)_____ is inaccurate and he's refusing to pay. The boot manufacturer is threatening to sue my client.

Did you come across any cases at the conference that might cover this situation? I'm wondering if this is a fundamental breach. What do you think? Can my client avoid the contract and not pay for the boots?

I'd be really grateful if you could get back to me as soon as possible. Cheers.
George

2 Read the details of a similar case that Harry has found. What are the similarities? Are there any differences? What do you think was the result of the case?

A Dutch seller and a German buyer entered into a contract for the sale of a product with special technical qualities. The buyer declared the contract avoided because the product delivered was of a lower quality than what was agreed in the contract. Also, the product was produced in South Africa and not in the UK, as had been stated in the contract. The seller had also given the buyer certificates of origin and quality that did not match Dutch regulations. The buyer exercised his right to avoid the contract. The seller did not accept the avoidance. The seller sued to recover the purchase price from the buyer.

3 a Read the ruling on the case in Exercise 2.

> **The German Supreme Court held:**
> - The buyer had not validly avoided the contract.
> - The seller was entitled to be awarded the full price.
> - They did not accept the buyer's argument that he was entitled to avoid the contract under Art. 49(1)(b) CISG

b Use the case details to write a memo from Harry to George, giving his opinion on what George's client should do.

USEFUL LANGUAGE

Comparing
In both cases, …
There are several similarities.
Whereas …
Although …
On one hand, we have …; On the other, …
Nevertheless, …
There's a marked difference/similarity between …

Conceding
While it might be said/argued that …
Granted …
Admittedly, …
We have to consider …
Naturally, …

Summarizing
In conclusion, …
All in all, …
To conclude, …
To sum up, …
In short, …
Consequently, …

5 Contract law 2

Reading: Part 3

TIP
Read the gapped sentences carefully to decide if you need a noun, verb, adjective, etc. If in doubt, think about some common endings for this type of word and make a guess. Read through the sentences or phrases afterwards in your head to see if they sound right.

Read this website extract about restitution. Use the words on the left to make one word that fits the numbered gap in the text.

1 CONTRACT
2 CONSIDER
3 HEAD
4 BASE
5 RESTRICT
6 SOLE
7 IMPROVE
8 EXPEND
9 EXPECT
10 PROFIT

Restitution

Restitution is where the claimant has conferred a benefit on the defendant in performing their (1)_____ duties and wants to claim that benefit back. An example of this is where the claimant has paid in advance for goods which have not been delivered.

The loss is measured with regard to the value of the actual benefit as opposed to the claimant's loss, but will only be permitted if there is a serious breach and a total failure of (2)_____.

The purpose of a claim under this (3)_____ is to put both parties into the position they would have been in had the contract never been entered into, although in some situations the claimant may be placed in a better position.

The claimant is entitled to choose the (4)_____ upon which to make their claim, but there are certain (5)_____. Where the claimant has made a 'bad bargain', they will not be able to claim damages by relying (6)_____ on the loss if it puts them in a better position than they would have been in had the contract been performed. In any event, it is for the defendant to prove that the claimant has made a bad bargain. In the case of *C.&P. Haulage v. Middleton (1983)*, the claimant had hired a garage for six months, and it was agreed that any (7)_____ would be the property of the defendant. When the defendant breached the contract, the claimant sued for the cost of these. The court held that even if the contract had not been breached, the (8)_____ would have been wasted.

In some situations, it may also be possible to recover twice for the same loss under the various bases as outlined above, as long as the loss itself is not duplicated.

In general, though, the claimant will seek damages assessed on the (9)_____ basis, as this usually proves to be more (10)_____.

Listening: Part 2

TIP
The words you need to complete each sentence will all be from the listening. However, the rest of each sentence may be phrased in a different way from the original. Read the sentences carefully before you listen and predict the type of information you are going to be listening for.

🎧 20 **5.2** You will hear a speaker giving a welcome and overview of a one-day conference on Contract and Commercial Law. Listen and complete the sentences.

Conference on Contract and Commercial Law
Being aware of latest developments in this field will help reduce (1)_____ for law firms and their clients.
The course has been designed to be intensive to assist those who have limited (2)_____.
The course is aimed at both (3)_____ and private-practice lawyers.
Participants will receive advice on dealing with (4)_____ contracts in particular.
One speaker today is well known because of his involvement in a case that turned on (5)_____.
'How to avoid expensive (6)_____' will be the focus of another session.
A very important concern for contract and commercial lawyers is drafting (7)_____ indemnities.
Participants will benefit from the (8)_____ and techniques of experts throughout the day.
Mr Frans Viedrict is the (9)_____ speaker of the day

5 Contract law 2

Writing: Part 1

TIP
Make sure you divide your letter into clear paragraphs so that the reader can follow your thoughts easily. Do not use language that is too colloquial.

You are a lawyer, and one of your clients, Milton Football Club, has been able to buy a player from Barford Football Club because of a special escape clause in the player's contract. Barford FC is unhappy about the situation.
Read the letter from Mr Trafford, from Barford FC, on which you have already made some handwritten notes. Then, using all the information in your handwritten notes, write a letter to Mr Trafford on behalf of your client, Milton FC.

Regarding the transfer of Player X from Barford FC to your club, it is clear that you breached the rules by contacting Player X directly. *[He contacted us – explain]* The rules state that you should have contacted us first. It is also clear that Player X leaked confidential information about the escape clause in his contract to you. *[Your wording – suggest more careful in future!]* This information that Barford FC was obliged to accept an offer of a minimum of 5.5 million pounds for Player X allowed you to buy him for at least 2 million pounds below his value. *[No – value exaggerated – indicate more realistic value]*

We are confident that if Player X had stayed with us, the club profits would have increased by 2 million pounds because of increased spectator numbers and television coverage. We are therefore claiming a further 2 million pounds from you in compensation. *[Disagree – request proof of expected loss]*

If you fail to agree to this, we shall take legal action. *[No legal responsibility, but suggest compromise – say what and why]*

Yours faithfully

Thomas Trafford

Write a letter of between 120 and 180 words in an appropriate style. Do not write any postal addresses.

Speaking: Part 2

TIP
If you have a problem thinking of enough to say about the topic, give some examples from your own experience or what happens in your country.

Look at these two topics. Select one of them and give a short talk on it for about a minute. There are some ideas to help you. You have a minute to prepare your talk. After you have finished your talk, your partner will ask you a brief question about it.

TASK 1

Breach of contract (1)
- Different types of breach
- Difficulty in proving a fundamental breach
- Importance of 'forseeability'

TASK 2

Breach of contract (2)
- Action that can be taken when breach suspected
- Remedies available
- Appropriateness of different types of damages

5 Contract law 2

6 Real property law

■ **Lead-in** Discuss this question with a partner.

What does *real property* mean?

Reading 1

Property law is the general term used to describe law relating to the different forms of ownership in real property such as land, as distinct from personal property or moveable property, within the common-law legal system. In the civil-law system, there is a division between movable and immovable property. Movable property equates to personal property, while immovable property is roughly the same as real estate or real property and the associated rights and obligations attaching to the land. The main distinction in common-law systems is between real property (land and what is sited on land) and personal property (chattels).

1 Read the extract on the left to check your answer to the Lead-in. What is *real property* called in your country?

2 Match the words in the box to the definitions below.

| easement | estate | freehold | heir | landlord | leasehold |
| licence | rent | tenant |

1 A type of interest in real property with different degrees of ownership recognized in law
2 An estate that is for a fixed period of time
3 The fullest form of right in land
4 A person who inherits property on another person's death
5 A person who leases land belonging to another person
6 The money paid by a lessee
7 A right enjoyed by someone over another's property; for example, a right of way
8 A power or authority passing no interest in the land but merely giving permission to use the land for a particular purpose
9 The owner of an estate or interest in property which has been leased to another party

3 a Discuss or research the meanings of the following expressions. Write a short definition for each in your own words.

1 fee simple
2 fee tail
3 life estate
4 estate per autre vie
5 reversion
6 remainder

b Work in pairs. Read your definitions for your partner to guess what you are describing.

Reading 2

1 Discuss these questions with a partner.

1 What legal problems related to real property do you think commercial lawyers have to deal with most often? Why?
2 What information would you expect to find on the website of a legal firm that specializes in real property? What would make one website more attractive than another? Why?

2 Read the webpage below which advertises a lawyer's services. Complete the gaps using these sentences.

a If you are evicting a tenant for the first time and the tenant is fighting the eviction with a lawyer, think twice.

b They can even be useful at the initial stage in advising you on choosing tenants and how to avoid such claims further down the road.

c Therefore the burden of proof is very high on landlords.

d They want to make their business profitable, while at the same time avoiding liability.

e If you are taken to court or if you have to settle, your liability can be much higher without legal representation.

If you are a property owner, then you can benefit from a lawyer's help.

Learn when you should consult a lawyer
When should a landlord hire a lawyer? Landlords are more or less the same as other types of business owner. **(1)**_____ In certain situations, it's a smart move to get in touch with a lawyer who will guide you on this. The following are some common scenarios that will benefit from a professional review or professional input.

Removing a tenant from your property
An eviction lawsuit can be quick and take less time than other civil-law actions. Landlords must follow detailed rules, from notifying the tenant of the lawsuit to filing the right papers and forms. Because it's the tenant's home, many judges might look more favourably on the tenant's submissions. **(2)**_____ Still, many landlords try to evict a tenant themselves, sometimes successfully and sometimes unsuccessfully. There are many occasions when you need to stop and think. **(3)**_____ If the tenant is an employee that you are firing, think twice. If you must comply with rent control or housing programme eviction rules, think twice. If the tenant is filing for bankruptcy, think twice.

If you are being investigated or sued for illegal discrimination then you can benefit from a lawyer's help
Landlords who do everything by the book and carefully comply with fair housing laws can still face accusations. You won't need a lawyer every time you are faced with these claims, but if a tenant is taking proceedings against you or a housing agency agrees to look into a claim, then you should definitely consult a lawyer. **(4)**_____ Another point to consider is that if you are involved in such a process and it becomes public, then it may well harm your business reputation. A lawyer can help you resolve the dispute, end the investigation or deal with the lawsuit as soon as possible. **(5)**_____

Language work

3 Match the verbs (1–8) with the phrases (a–h) to complete the collocations from the webpage.

1 file	a liability
2 take	b more favourably on
3 look	c the right papers
4 consult	d proceedings against
5 resolve	e a lawyer
6 notify	f into a claim
7 avoid	g the dispute
8 look	h the tenant

4 Discuss these questions with a partner.

1 Why do you think some landlords might choose *not* to use a lawyer? Are there any advantages to this?

2 In your country, what is the procedure for evicting a tenant? Is the law generally more favourable to the tenant or the landlord?

Writing

1 Work in pairs. Write a short paragraph for your firm's website. Say why clients should choose to consult you about their real property problems. Use some of the expressions in the Useful language box.

> **USEFUL LANGUAGE**
> Here at ... , we ...
> For many years, we ...
> As a result, our experience enables us to ...
> Our speciality is ...
> You just have to look at our results!
> Not only do we ... , but ...
> We can cater for ...
> Here are excerpts from testimonials from some of our clients: ...

2 Read your classmates' paragraphs. Which would *you* consult, and why?

Listening

1 Work in pairs. A woman, Mrs Grant, and her son want to lease a commercial premises to operate two businesses from. What will the lawyer have to consider when drawing up the commercial lease?

2 🎧 21 6.1 Listen to a phone conversation between Mrs Grant and her lawyer, Mr Hockney. Complete these notes.

- ★ Mrs Grant wants Mr Hockney to give her (1) _____ _____ and to negotiate commercial leases.

- ★ After the conversation, she will send him the (2) _____ _____ .

- ★ Mrs Grant must decide the amount she wishes to give as a (3) _____ _____ .

- ★ Utilities can be paid for in two ways: (4) _____ or included (5) _____ _____ _____ .

- ★ In the lease, there must be:
  - provision for ending (6) _____ _____ _____ if their businesses expand;
  - provision for (7) _____ if they have financial problems;.
  - correct (8) _____ to allow one to sublet to the other if necessary.

- ★ Mr Hockney is going to:
  - (9) _____ a letter to send to the agent;
  - write to Mrs Grant (10) _____ what has been discussed.

6 Real property law

3 🎧 **21** **6.1** Listen to the recording again or read the audio transcript (page 100) and find informal equivalents for these words and expressions in the conversation.

1 starting my own business
2 complement each other
3 contact me again
4 calculate
5 a portion of
6 apportioned
7 equip
8 conduct
9 are unsuccessful
10 written
11 explain again
12 cease trading
13 start the process
14 get in touch

4 Write the letter from Mr Hockney to Mrs Grant confirming the points covered in the conversation. Will you use the formal or informal equivalents? Why?

- Read the audio transcript (page 100) and make relevant notes.
- Group the points into paragraphs.
- Explain in the first paragraph why you are writing.
- Expand your notes in the main paragraphs.
- Conclude by clarifying what you both need to do next.
- Check your letter for content/organization/accuracy.

Language work

5 🎧 **21** **6.1** Work in pairs. Cover the Useful language box below. Mr Hockney used a sequence of phrases to introduce different points in his conversation. How many can you remember? Listen again or read the audio transcript (page 100) and write them down.

> **USEFUL LANGUAGE**
> Firstly, …
> We also need to consider …
> Also, …
> Another factor we need to consider …
> And, of course, …
> There's something else, too: …
> And – oh yes! – …
> We mustn't forget …
> And one more thing: …
> That's about it for the moment.

Speaking

Using some of the phrases in the Useful language box, prepare to talk for two minutes about what steps a person needs to take when buying a property in your country.

Reading 3

1 Work in pairs. What do these terms mean? Check your answers in a dictionary.

1 title insurance
2 risk management
3 financial backing
4 professional negligence
5 lending institution
6 single premium
7 standard tool

2 Read this messaging exchange between two lawyers and decide whether the statements below are true (T) or false (F).

> **George Burns says:**
> Hans, I remembered that you're an expert in title insurance. I've got a client who wants to buy an apartment complex in the Baltics – Latvia, to be precise. I remember you talking about title insurance, and from what I recall, you're a real expert at this – or at least much better informed than I am! Have you got a moment to help me out?
>
> **Hans Brecht says:**
> Sure, although I wouldn't say I was an expert! But I do have a fair amount of experience in that area. In Germany, we don't have any real need for it, as registration of the title is presumed to be a valid title. But in the Baltics, it's used quite a lot – in fact, I always recommend it to clients who are investing in any of the Baltic states. It's a risk-management product which means that buyers and lenders benefit from a clean ownership title. It's good, too, from a lawyer's perspective in that it means that we don't have to worry about professional negligence claims.
>
> **George Burns says:**
> That's great, Hans. What exactly does title insurance do?
>
> **Hans Brecht says:**
> OK. For a single premium, typically the insurance covers any loss that might arise from title flaws and other problems relating to real estate – you know, things like local authority regulations and land-use permits. Actually, when it was first introduced, or rather became available, the insurance only covered 'unknown defects', namely defects or problems in the title that would have been unknown to the buyer. This was a bit of a problem for the lending institutions, so now the insurance covers known and unknown defects. Now it's a standard tool used worldwide to insure title risks in real estate and it's widely used by lenders – so your client will find it much easier to get financial backing from a financial institution if he has it in place. Is that what you need?
>
> **George Burns says:**
> That's excellent – thanks, Hans! Any time I can return the favour, just let me know!

1 George's client has purchased property in Latvia.
2 Hans often uses his expertise in title insurance in Germany.
3 The people who profit most from title insurance are the sellers of property.
4 There has been a change to what is covered by title insurance.
5 Having title insurance has no effect on funding for property projects.

3 **Complete these sentences using words from the messages. Try not to look back at the messages.**

1 It's good, too, from a lawyer's _____ .
2 It's easier to get financial backing if a client has this in _____ .
3 From what I _____ , you're a real expert!
4 Just let me know if I can _____ the favour.
5 Have you got a _____ to help me out?
6 I've got a _____ amount of experience.

Writing

1 **Using the information from the messages on the opposite page and the notes below, write a letter to your client summarizing the benefits of getting title insurance. Use some of the phrases from the Useful language box.**

> **USEFUL LANGUAGE**
> Not only can you … , but …
> There's an added advantage in that …
> An important benefit is that …
> Another reason to seriously consider taking out title insurance is that …
> You won't lose out because …
> I should also inform you that …

- Users of title insurance include investors, property developers, foreign banks, property sellers
- One-off premium, which can be adjusted in the event of an increase of the value of the property
- Cover for risks in respect of title issues
- Any litigation covered
- Indemnifies against a judgement up to the amount covered by the insurance
- Owner always guaranteed never to lose the amount insured because of any problems with the title
- Cost of insurance depends on size of the property deal and level of complication (usually between about 0.2% and 0.5% of the total value of the transaction)

Research

2 **Work with a partner. Research another topic related to real property you can advise your partner on, then role-play another message exchange between George Burns and Hans Brecht. George is returning the favour by giving Hans some information he needs. Exchange written messages. You are not allowed to talk!**

'Hello, I'd like to apply for some property insurance.'

6 Real property law

Reading: Part 6

Read this article from an online magazine about buying property in Spain and the questions. For each question, choose the best answer: A, B, C or D.

What are the pitfalls of buying property in Spain?

If you're thinking of buying property in Spain, be aware that the whole process can be fraught with pitfalls ... but that's only if you fail to take a few sensible precautions. All too often, foreign buyers plunge headlong into signing on the dotted line without giving enough consideration to the fine print and a host of factors that need to be taken into account when purchasing property in a country where the language, customs and bureaucracy are all unfamiliar.

Bizarrely, many foreigners are still buying Spanish properties without the benefit of legal advice – even though they would probably never consider being so foolhardy in their own country. The lure of all that sunshine, cheap wine and easy living just seems to go to the heads of otherwise fairly level-headed individuals.

Couples will quite happily sign an initial purchase agreement after a weekend inspection visit financed, or part-funded, by a developer or estate agent. It's only later that they realize they were subjected to unacceptably high-pressure (even aggressive) sales pitches, that the property they've committed themselves to is wholly inappropriate and that the location is entirely unsuitable for their needs.

Agents aren't normally the kind of people to warn you about the floods, fires and earthquake damage that your chosen area is particularly prone to. You think we're being unnecessarily alarmist? No, these are all problems that can and do occur on a regular basis in certain parts of Spain, and to be forewarned is to be forearmed.

Fools can rush into a minefield of legal problems in Spain. Many foreigners have bought properties, only to find the vendor is not the true owner, the property comes with hefty debts on it or an apartment block is about to be constructed nearby totally blocking out your much-prized sea view. These things can and *do* happen on a regular basis.

Buyers who go for 'off-plan' properties (i.e. buying into a development before it has actually been built) have encountered all sorts of disasters. Sometimes developers go bust before the project is completed, sometimes the completion date is long overdue and the original specifications are not adhered to – you might even find the developer has already mortgaged the property before you even secured your option to buy!

There are a couple of simple steps you can take to guard against most problems that arise for foreign buyers. The most important thing is to hire a good, reputable lawyer who speaks your language and who specializes in the Spanish property market. He or she will protect you against all the potential legal problems that can arise. The second thing is to visit your chosen area several times, at different times of the year, before you commit to buying and, if at all possible, rent a property for at least a few weeks before you make your final decision.

TIP
Read the text first so that you understand the general idea. Then look at the questions. Sometimes you may have an idea of the answer before looking at the options.

1 The people who encounter problems buying property in Spain ...
 A ... have often had similar experiences in their own countries.
 B ... usually use the wrong lawyer.
 C ... would not usually make bad decisions when buying property.
 D ... don't consider the legal aspects.

2 Houses in Spain are often sold ...
 A ... through high-powered selling techniques.
 B ... without being inspected carefully enough.
 C ... after buyers have paid a small deposit.
 D ... to buyers who don't really want the commitment.

3 According to the article, ...
 A ... some reports exaggerate the problems faced by new owners.
 B ... estate agents and developers sometimes lie about the dangers.
 C ... buyers are usually made aware of potential problems.
 D ... it is better for buyers to have more information about possible dangers.

4 What sort of legal problems can buyers face?
 A It is difficult to identify the real owner of the property.
 B The buyer cannot sell the property on.
 C A search doesn't reveal future developments.
 D The buyer's level of debt can increase rapidly.

5 When buying uncompleted developments, ...
 A ... buyers should check out the developers' records.
 B ... buyers can change their minds regarding building specifications.
 C ... buyers sometimes need to take out a second mortgage.
 D ... there's a risk that the developers may not keep to the deal.

6 When buying property abroad, it's important to ...
 A ... speak the language.
 B ... hire a specialist lawyer.
 C ... do a lot of research.
 D ... consider renting instead of buying.

Speaking: Part 3

TIP
In this part of the test, you are expected to interact, not take turns to give your ideas. It's important to ask what your partner thinks and comment on his/her ideas.

A client has a problem with a residential tenant. He suspects that the tenant is subletting part of the property to a third party, who is operating a business. Advise your client about the situation.

Discussion points
- The difficulty of proving that this is happening
- The terms of the lease
- Advisability of settling the dispute outside court
- Possible legal steps to take

Listening: Part 2

TIP
The first time you listen, it's important to understand the general meaning and not to worry too much about details, as you may miss the next sections. You can check the details the second time you listen.

🎧 22 **6.2** You are going to hear a conversation between Brigitte Trant, a helpline advisor, and Thomas Maine, who is planning to set up a business abroad. Choose the best answer: A, B or C.

1. Thomas needs advice on …
   A … which aspects of the transaction he needs a lawyer for.
   B … finding a suitable lawyer to represent him.
   C … how to protect his interests once the business is operating.
2. According to the advisor, how many lawyers does he need?
   A She doesn't give a definite answer.
   B Several specialist lawyers
   C One good lawyer with a range of experience
3. How can some societies help him?
   A They can recommend the best lawyers.
   B They can research the lawyers for him.
   C They can give some information about suitable lawyers.
4. What should Thomas consider when choosing a lawyer?
   A They look knowledgeable.
   B They've been in the country for a long time.
   C They communicate well with people.
5. The advisor says that he shouldn't use a lawyer …
   A … who doesn't reveal his/her fees.
   B … who advertises in property sale magazines.
   C … recommended by someone involved in the transaction.

Writing: Part 2

TIP
Plan your memo first by making notes for the different paragraphs. Sometimes writing notes can bring ideas and clarify your thoughts.

You are a senior partner in a law firm that specializes in real property law. You want to extend the firm's website. Write a memo to colleagues asking them to submit articles on different aspects of real property law for inclusion on the website.

- Explain the purpose of the articles
- Outline topic areas for the articles
- Express preference for certain areas, with reasons
- Advise on length, style and schedule for submissions

Write your answer in 200–250 words.

7 Company law 1

Lead-in

Discuss these questions with a partner.
1 What are the main types of company?
2 What are the features of each different type of company?

Listening 1

1 🎧 23 **7.1** A client, Charles, is asking his lawyer, Kate, about setting up a company in the UK. Listen to the first part of the discussion and answer these questions.
1 Has Charles been involved in setting up a company before?
2 What is Charles's business?
3 Where does Charles want to set up his business?
4 What will the company do?
5 Who will its main competition be?

2 **Read Kate's explanation about the different types of company. Check your ideas from the Lead-in.**

In essence, there are four main types of company. First, we have a private company limited by shares, which has a share capital. The liability of each member is limited to the amount unpaid on shares that a member holds. A private company cannot offer its shares for sale to the general public. Then there's a private company limited by guarantee. In this company, members do not make any contribution to the capital during its lifetime, as they do not purchase shares, and the member's liability is limited to the amount that they each agree to contribute to the company's assets if it is wound up. Thirdly, there's a private unlimited company. Here, the company may or may not have a share capital, and there is no limit to the members' liability. Because of this, the company has to disclose less information than other types of companies. Finally, there is the public limited company. This type has a share capital, and the liability is limited to the amount unpaid on shares that a member holds. A public limited company may offer its shares for sale to the general public and may also be quoted on the stock exchange.

3 a **Cover the text in Exercise 2. Write brief notes about each of the four different types of company. Use these words.**

general   liability   limited   private   share   public

b **Compare with a partner and check against the text in Exercise 2.**

4 **Discuss what you think are the advantages and disadvantages of the different types of company. Which type of company do you think would be most suitable for Charles? Why?**

Reading 1

1 Use these facts (a–h) to complete the table below summarizing the different types of business entities.

a Articles of Association must be clearly set out and filed with the appropriate authority.
b Can terminate on death.
c Legal fees of registration
d May be dissolved, depending on the agreement terms.
e Minimal cost
f Names of partners need not be disclosed to public.
g Same as general partnerships, except that the interests are usually deemed securities.
h Shared or centralized, depending on agreement

type of company factors	sole proprietorship	general partnerships	limited partnerships	limited liability
ease of formation	No legal formalities	Written document not required, but usually advisable.	Certificate of Limited Partnership must be signed by all partners. May be some filing requirements.	(7) _____
cost of formation	(1) _____	Drafting the partnership agreement and official recording.	Time-consuming drafting and associated costs.	(8) _____
raising capital	Personal responsibility	Loans to partnership and partners' own capital contributions are main sources.	(5) _____	Flexibility in raising capital.
management and control	Centred in one person	(3) _____	General partners, but limited partners must be excluded from control to retain limited liability.	Can have a board of directors with extensive powers.
owners' liability	Owner subject to personal liability for obligations and liabilities	Partners usually share risks, according to the partnership agreement.	General partners have unlimited liability; limited partners are limited to loss of their agreed capital contribution.	Liability is limited to the original capital investment of the members and formalities have to be followed.
continuity of business	(2) _____	(4) _____	No guarantee of unlimited duration. May be dissolved due to loss of limited partners.	Dissolution process needs to be stated, as statutory requirements apply.
other advantages	Freedom to do business anywhere without restrictions	Ease of operation, as terms are agreed between the partners.	(6) _____	Most flexible of entities, as members can set out their terms of operation, though they are regulated by statute.

Language work

2 Find synonyms in the completed table for these words and phrases.

1 very wide
2 length
3 ending
4 very low
5 called/considered
6 end
7 keep
8 takes a lot of time
9 ended

3 Work in pairs. Choose an entity and talk about it for a minute. Summarize the good and bad points. Ask your partner a question about his/her talk.

Reading 2

1 a Quickly read the three extracts below, ignoring the gaps. Then match each extract (A–C) with one of these types of document (1–3).

   1 An agreement   2 An EC recommendation   3 A statute

b Which modal verbs are typically used in each type of document?

Extract A

The structure of directors' remuneration should promote the long-term **(1)** _____ of the company and ensure that remuneration is based on performance. Variable components of remuneration should therefore be **(2)** _____ to predetermined and measurable performance criteria, including criteria of a **(3)** _____ nature. Limits should be set on the variable components of remuneration. Significant variable components of remuneration should be deferred for a **(4)** _____ period, for example, three to five years, subject **(5)** _____ performance conditions. Further, companies should be able to reclaim variable components of remuneration that were paid on the basis of data, which proved to be **(6)** _____ misstated.

Extract B

The memorandum of a company limited by guarantee must **(7)** _____ state that each member undertakes to **(8)** _____ to the assets of the company in the event of its being wound up **(9)** _____ he is a member, or within one year after he ceases to be a member, for payment of the debts and liabilities of the company contracted before he ceases to be a member, and of the costs, charges and debts of winding up, and for **(10)** _____ of the rights of the contributories among themselves, **(11)** _____ amount as may be required, not exceeding a **(12)** _____ amount.

Extract C

The partners shall have equal rights in the management of the partnership business, and each partner shall **(13)** _____ their entire time to the conduct of the business. Without the **(14)** _____ of the other partner, neither partner shall **(15)** _____ behalf of the partnership borrow or lend money, or make, deliver, or accept any **(16)** _____ paper, or execute any mortgage, security agreement, bond, or lease, or purchase or contract to purchase, or sell or contract to sell any property for or of the partnership **(17)** _____ than the type of property bought and sold in the regular course of **(18)** _____ business

2 Work in pairs. Read the extracts again and complete the gaps with the words below. Think about the types of words you need to fit the grammar of the sentences.

Extract A: certain   linked   manifestly   non-financial   sustainability   to

Extract B: adjustment   also   contribute   specified   such   while

Extract C: commercial   consent   devote   its   on   other

3 Imagine you are rewriting the extracts above in plain English. How would you replace these words?

Extract A
1 remuneration   2 ensure   3 significant   4 deferred   5 further   6 reclaim
7 manifestly

Extract B
8 undertakes   9 ceases   10 exceeding

Extract C
11 their entire time   12 execute   13 purchase

Reading 3

1 You are going to read about roles in company management. Before you read, discuss with a partner what you know about these roles.

1 a shareholder   2 a director   3 the company secretary

2 Read this text and check your ideas to Exercise 1.

Shareholders – or 'members' – of a company are those people who have legal ownership of a share and appear in the company's register. These people may not actually have beneficial ownership, but simply be a 'nominee'. However, unless otherwise stated in the company's articles, only the shareholder himself can exercise the rights attached to holding his shares. These include the right to vote and to receive dividends. They also include the ability to enforce rights against the company. It is the shareholders who own a company, and they control what the company does. They can appoint and remove directors and change the company articles. A shareholder's rights are set out in the articles and supported by the Companies Act.

The directors of a company are chosen by the shareholders, and their job is to manage the company and decide general policy. In smaller companies, directors themselves choose how long to remain in position, unless they are forced out. In larger, listed companies, however, it is normal for directors to retire and stand for election annually at the AGM. This is usually a formality. The law states that all directors of listed companies should stand for re-election at least every three years. Directors act on behalf of the shareholders and should never use the company's assets as they wish. To this end, their powers to run the company are limited by law and the company's constitution. A company will have both executive and non-executive directors. The difference is that whereas the executive director is employed by the company and given specific contractual duties, the non-executive director is not an employee and receives a fee rather than a salary. He is not usually full time and is not involved in the day-to-day running of the company. Both types of director, however, have the same legal responsibilities. Certain people, such as the under-sixteens and bankrupts, are not allowed by law to become directors of a company, but the upper age limit of 70 has recently been removed.

The Company Secretary is the chief administrative officer of a company and is appointed or removed by the board of directors. He will normally have appropriate formal qualifications, relevant experience and expertise. He is responsible to the whole board, not only the Chairman or Chief Executive. The role is very important in a company, and the duties are wide ranging and can change from one company to another. Generally, the Company Secretary is responsible for accounting and finance and dealing with personnel. However, with recent increased interest in corporate governance, the Company Secretary is now seen as the guardian of the company's compliance with both law and best practice. This includes responsibility for compliance with employment legislation, security of documentation, insurance, etc.

3 Read the text again and decide whether these statements are true or false.

1 People with beneficial ownership have the same rights as shareholders.
2 Directors are answerable to the shareholders.
3 Directors of all companies must stand for re-election every three years.
4 Both executive and non-executive directors are employees of a company.
5 People over 70 can continue to be directors.
6 The Company Secretary is chosen by the shareholders.
7 The Company Secretary's responsibilities are to the Chairman or Chief Executive.
8 It is the Company Secretary's job to ensure that the company complies with legislation.

Listening 2

1 a Charles's lawyer, Kate, is giving him some more advice about what type of company he should form. Here are some of the things he mentions. In pairs, discuss what you know about each of them.

1 community interest company
2 asset lock
3 Memorandum of Association
4 Articles of Association

b 🎧 24 7.2 Listen and note what you hear about the different things.

2 🎧 24 7.2 Listen again. Who says each of the phrases in the Useful language box, Charles (C) or Kate (K)? In each case, what are they referring to?

USEFUL LANGUAGE

1 You should be thinking about …
2 You should give some thought to …
3 This could well be appropriate for …
4 That's up to you to decide.
5 It would be really useful if you could send us …
6 We can go through it.
7 We'll put our heads together.
8 You can set the necessary paperwork in motion.
9 I'll have to look into this further.
10 If you come back to me …
11 I'll get going on …

Writing

1 a Below is Charles's letter to Kate with queries about setting up a community interest company. What questions do you think he will ask?

b Read the letter to check.

> Dear Kate,
>
> Further to our conversation at your office last week, I've been speaking to my brothers, and we've got a few questions about the community interest company. We're not sure whether what we're hoping to do will actually qualify as a community interest company.
>
> As I told you, we want to set up an engineering company to provide water-drilling equipment, training and expertise to those in developing countries. So, we need to know whether such a company can only operate for the benefit of a community in the UK. Secondly, how do they actually define 'community' for the purposes of a community investment company? Does the community extend to those in developing countries? Thirdly, how does such a company differ from an ordinary company? Fourthly, how are CICs financed, and are there any restrictions on financing them? Finally, what are our duties to members, third parties and to Companies House?
>
> As soon as you have this information, we would be grateful if you could send it on to us so that we can make an informed decision.
>
> I look forward to hearing from you at your convenience.
>
> Best wishes,
>
> Charles

2 Kate has made the following notes about CICs. Use them to write a letter to Charles, answering his questions. Remember to expand and link the notes in your letter. You will have to be selective about the notes you use.

---

1 **Registration**
- Memorandum and Articles of Association for CIC must have letters 'CIC' at end of name
- must have an asset lock in Articles of Association – property and assets – used solely or mainly for objects – can't be disposed of except to charity or other CIC
- big difference to other companies – cap on distribution of profits to investors as dividends
- managed by directors – only limited powers to members or shareholders
- reasonable limits on directors' salaries and benefits – must make operating for the 'benefit of the community' transparent

2 **Benefit of community**
- regulator decides each application
- support of community projects – considered
- contracting to provide services – use surpluses for benefit of community

3 **Community**
- residents of town or district
- people in town or district with needs
- groups of people overseas in developing countries with needs
- not family; group of friends; employees of particular business; members of club

4 **Financing**
- access to grants and soft loans – not available to private-sector business
- self-financing – inward investment and trading – issues of shares with limited dividends – loans with limited interest – issuing debentures secured on its assets

5 **Duties to members**
- act honestly – conduct business with reasonable degree of care and skill
- prepare annual reports – directors must declare personal financial interests in company's dealings – all directors must act within their powers and the objects of the company

---

Speaking

Work in pairs. You want to set up a company. Decide what your business is going to be, then change partners. Role-play the conversation about setting up the company, with your new partner playing the role of your lawyer. Use the phrases from Listening 2, Exercise 2 on the opposite page.

Reading: Part 1

Read the first part of an article about company meetings.
For each question 1–6, choose the best word or phrase to fill each gap from A, B, C or D below.

Board meetings

The articles of a company will **(1)** _____ the management of the company to its board of directors. The board will act collectively, meeting regularly to consider and decide **(2)** _____ affecting the company. How those board meetings are run is a matter **(3)** _____ for the articles and for the board itself to decide. Unlike shareholders' meetings, which are more tightly regulated, board meetings are generally **(4)** _____ of legislative interference.

So there is nothing in statute about the notice to be given for board meetings. Any director or the secretary can call a board meeting and, unless the articles or a previous board meeting have stipulated the length of notice to be given, the only **(5)** _____ is that it be reasonable.

What is reasonable will depend on the type of company and its past practice. For a private company where all directors are already on site, reasonable notice may be a few hours or even minutes; for a large international company with directors scattered over the globe and non-executives with other responsibilities, board meetings will be fixed a year or more in **(6)** _____ . Again, unless the articles or a board resolution say anything to the contrary, the notice can be written or oral and need not detail an agenda for the meeting.

TIP
Make sure that your choice of word collocates with the word coming before or after the gap. Sometimes you need to look beyond the words immediately following the gap to find a clue. Always read through the whole sentence.

1	A pass	B deliver	C delegate	D convert
2	A ideas	B issues	C problems	D influences
3	A largely	B mostly	C preferably	D importantly
4	A absent	B unrestricted	C free	D closed
5	A need	B restriction	C requirement	D demand
6	A advance	B future	C anticipation	D ahead

Read the second part of the article about company meetings.
For questions 7–12, choose the best word or phrase to fill each gap from A, B, C or D below.

Notice

All shareholders are entitled to receive written notice of a meeting unless the articles say **(7)** _____ (a smaller company's articles may often state that notice is only to be given to those shareholders who have provided a UK address to the company). In **(8)** _____ , notice of a general meeting must also be given to each director (**(9)** _____ a shareholder or not) and to the auditors – a point that can often be missed. The articles will state how notice can be given to shareholders, and it is important that their provisions are followed: failure to do so can **(10)** _____ the notice, the meeting and the resolutions passed at it.

Legislation introduced in 2000 allows notices to be sent electronically (by email or fax) if a shareholder is in **(11)** _____ . Since January 2007, a company has also been able to use a website.
Documents and information to be sent to shareholders can be posted on a website if a shareholder resolution allowing this has been passed (or the articles permit it). Shareholders can **(12)** _____ out and still require hard copies through the post. In any event, each time a document is put on the website, shareholders must be told, usually by hard-copy letter.

7	A alternatively	B opposite	C otherwise	D different
8	A extra	B fact	C advance	D addition
9	A if	B whether	C maybe	D conditionally
10	A negate	B illegalize	C invalidate	D deny
11	A acceptance	B agreement	C understanding	D accord
12	A choose	B make	C opt	D go

7 Company law 1

Speaking: Part 4

TIP
Try to extend your answers beyond just one sentence, but remember that it is not an opportunity for you to talk for a long time. If you have opinions or something to say about a question your partner is asked, wait until he/she has finished speaking, then make your comment.

Answer these questions.
1 What is the role of a director of a company?
2 What are the advantages and disadvantages of forming a partnership?
3 How and why might a director be removed?
4 What legal considerations are there for company management if a company operates in several different countries?

Listening: Part 4

TIP
Don't worry if you can't do both tasks after the first listening. Some students prefer to concentrate on the first task with the first listening, then focus on the second task when they listen again. Remember to listen to each speaker carefully to understand the idea of what he/she is saying and don't focus on only one or two sentences.

🎧 25–29 **7.3** You will hear five short extracts in which lawyers are talking to clients who are directors of companies.

TASK 1
For questions 1–5, choose from the list A–F what each director wants to do.

A leave the board for reasons of ill health
B set up a new company
C continue in his position
D remove the Company Secretary
E get involved in another business
F continue a business arrangement after leaving a company

TASK 2
For questions 6–10, choose from the list A–F what each lawyer is doing.

A offering reassurance
B reminding
C changing opinion
D regretting
E offering an alternative
F agreeing with a plan of action

Writing: Part 2

TIP
Invent a scenario for a case that you are familiar with. Remember that you have to write about an imaginary business and imaginary people, but these can be based on reality.

You work for a law firm and are going away on sick leave for several months. You are updating a colleague on one of your cases. Your client wants to form a partnership with two colleagues.

Write a memorandum to your colleague. Your memorandum should:
- explain why you have advised forming a partnership rather than a company
- describe the advice you have given your client on the obligations and liabilities of the partners
- outline what action you have taken to set up the partnership
- outline the next steps to take.

Write your answer in 200–250 words.

8 Company law 2

■ **Lead-in** Discuss these questions with a partner.
1 Why might a company restructure?
2 What are the different forms of restructuring called?

Reading 1

1 Quickly read the article on the opposite page to check your answers to the Lead-in.

2 Read the article again and choose the best alternatives to complete it.

3 Read the article again, then cover it and answer these questions.
1 What does company restructuring usually depend on?
2 Whose contractual relationships are changed?
3 What are the warning signs of poor financial performance?
4 How can bankruptcy breathe new life into a business?
5 How can a business restructure to expand?
6 When might an equity spin-off be beneficial?

Language work

4 Complete these sentences with appropriate words from the article.
1 Restructuring depends on the _____ economic conditions.
2 What is the _____ value of the company?
3 In _____ times, companies have to think carefully about whether to expand or not.
4 _____ sales are one indication of poor financial performance.
5 In an extreme situation, companies may _____ on their debts.
6 Competitive auctions are used to sell off _____ assets.

5 Complete these sentences in your own words.
1 There were significant accounting losses, so the company _____ .
2 The company was looking for new business opportunities and decided to _____ .
3 An equity spin-off was considered because _____ .

72   8 Company law 2

Company restructuring

Company restructuring is usually **(1)** *a response / an answer* from the company to **(2)** *extend / expand*, merge or downsize, depending on the economic circumstances prevailing. The important thing for a company is the **(3)** *timing / punctuality* of the restructuring. Company restructuring can be defined **(4)** *as / by* a process through which a company significantly changes the contractual relationships that exist among its creditors, shareholders, employees and other stakeholders. Usually, the goal of restructuring is to increase the **(5)** *overall / general* market value of the business enterprise. However, in recessionary times, the goal may be different, and the focus may be on trying to **(6)** *keep / maintain* the company's effectiveness and profitability. Some warning signs are obvious and need to be taken seriously. One may be the need to **(7)** *remedy / cure* poor financial performance. The warning signs are usually pretty clear: declining or stagnating sales, accounting losses or a **(8)** *reducing / falling* stock price. Defaulting on debts, resulting in bankruptcy, may occur in more extreme situations. Restructuring the debt can be difficult and costly. In some cases, however, legal processes are available that can greatly **(9)** *accelerate / speed up* the process. In the US, for example, bankruptcy can also be used to breathe new life into a business. Companies are allowed, for example, in a bankruptcy to **(10)** *refuse / reject* unfavourable leases or sell unwanted assets in a competitive auction. On the other hand, another reason to restructure is as a result of a new corporate strategy or to **(11)** *follow / take* advantage of a business opportunity. Such restructuring may involve expansion, including mergers, consolidations, acquisitions and various other activities which result in an enlargement of a firm or its **(12)** *scope / width* of operations. For example, diversified firms' businesses may be split into independent entities, each with its own common stock. In this case, there is an equity **(13)** *spin-off / spin-out*. These can be beneficial when high-growth business is being held **(14)** *back / down* by a parent company. One sign here is when the stock market is valuing the **(15)** *complete / entire* company for less than if it were split into separate entities.

The options available are frequently dependant on each individual company's circumstances and the prevailing market in which the company **(16)** *performs / operates*.

Reading 2

1 Discuss these questions with a partner.
1 What may a lawyer have to do when dealing with private individuals who have debtor/creditor problems?
2 What constitutes a partnership?
3 What do you know about the liabilities of partners for debts of the partnership?
4 What do you know about the liabilities of shareholders and directors for debts of a limited company?

2 Read the article on the opposite page to check your answers.

Language work

3 Use a dictionary to check and explain the difference between these pairs of expressions.
1 to wind up / to write off
2 in the case of / in respect of
3 to dissolve / to go bankrupt
4 jointly retained / a joint venture
5 personal guarantee / liability
6 debt / judgement
7 assets / profits
8 in relation to / to the extent of
9 regarded as / construed as

4 Choose the correct alternatives to complete these sentences.
1 My responsibilities range *about* / *from* dealing with insolvency cases *at* / *to* advising on mergers.
2 Lawyers often act *of* / *for* creditors regarding confirmation of the amounts owed.
3 The judgement can often go *against* / *counter* persons without good representation.
4 People are regarded *as* / *like* partners if they fulfil certain conditions.
5 The bankruptcy of one partner can mean that his debt will be written *over* / *off*.

5 a Match the halves of these phrases.

1 realize   a venture
2 jointly   b judgement
3 the lifetime   c and severally
4 the entry of   d the amount
5 a joint   e of a business entity

b Write five sentences of your own to show their meanings.

6 Read the article again and make brief notes on the main points of each paragraph. Then, using just your notes, rewrite the information in your own words.

Research

7 Research a recent high-profile insolvency case in your country and tell your partner about it.

Lawyers' involvement in maintaining a business entity

During the course of the lifetime of a business entity, many legal situations may be encountered which require the professional experience or assistance of a lawyer or legal professional. These may range from dealing with debtors and creditors, and the refinancing and restructuring of a business entity through mergers and acquisitions, to more serious situations related to insolvency and winding-up.

While the law in respect of debtors and creditors is an area that may involve a private individual or business entity, a lawyer's involvement in the legal aspects of debtors and creditors for a business entity are somewhat different from his/her involvement for a private individual. In the case of a private individual debtor, a lawyer may be required to either defend the debtor or act for a creditor in relation to: the accuracy of the amount claimed; the entry of judgement against the debtor by the creditor; the registration of the judgement against the debtor's property; and proceedings for the sale of the property of the debtor to realize the amount of the judgement for the creditor.

In the case of business entities, there may be some similarities in a lawyer's involvement, but the expertise and experience would be quite different, and the results may also have different consequences for the business entities compared to those of a private individual. In a partnership, for example, all partners are jointly and severally liable for all debts of the partnership to the full extent of their assets. If a partner gives a personal guarantee or a legal charge to a bank as security for the business debts, he/she should make sure that the bank accepts that they are only responsible for any debt incurred before the partnership is dissolved. If one partner goes bankrupt, although the debt will be written off for that partner, creditors can still pursue the remaining partners (or former partners) for the whole debt. In effect, what this means is that partners with the most assets have the most to lose.

If one partner has had to pay a partnership debt, that partner has the right to sue other partners for their share of the debt. A lawyer may be involved in relation to the question as to whether a partnership actually exists. Usually if there is no written agreement, and two or more persons are carrying on business with goal of making a profit, a partnership may be deemed to be in existence. However, persons who are not partners in other business transactions, but share the profits of one transaction, can be regarded as partners for that transaction. If, for example, two lawyers, who are not partners, come together and are jointly retained to act in a case and they agree to share the profits from acting in the case, then they could be deemed to be partners as far as the case is concerned. So a partnership may be limited to one situation, but the rights and liabilities of partners are the same as those applying to ordinary partnerships. A joint venture in respect of a single transaction may be construed as a partnership.

In a limited company, on the other hand, the shareholders are only liable for company debts to the extent of any unpaid sums due on their shares. Unless directors have given personal guarantees, they are not liable for the company's debts, so long as they run the company lawfully.

'Congratulations on becoming a partner – your share of company losses is £200,000.'

Reading 3

1 A lawyer is giving a pro-bono talk to a group on the basic types of shares and the advantages and disadvantages of investing in each type. Look at the slides he is using in the presentation and discuss the differences between these types of shares.

A

Redeemable non-voting shares

- No powers are given to the holders
- Directors can take them back at nominal value
- Can be used as reward for employees and are paid as dividends
- Useful if employee leaves or company is sold

B

Preference shares

- Usually have a preferential right to a fixed amount of dividend, if not a participating preference
- A 7% share will pay a dividend of 7p
- Only payable out of profits, but dividend may be more than fixed amount under complex rules
- May be given priority on return of capital
- Usually not entitled to share in surplus capital

C

Deferred ordinary shares

- Other classes of shares receive minimum dividend first
- Afterwards, they are fully participating
- Have advantages and disadvantages, depending on the shareholders' and the company's perspective

D

Management shares

- A type or class of shares with extra voting rights
- Useful to retain control of the company
- May confer multiple voting rights to each individual share or lower nominal value for each share
- Usually used after extra shares have been issued to outside investors

E

Other classes of shares

- Any class may be created, depending on the circumstances
- For example, in a joint venture with two companies and three investors (A, B and C), the companies may have three types of share
- 'A' shares, 'B' shares and 'C' shares may carry the same rights to protect the investors
- Articles may provide for nomination of a director for each class of share

2 Read this transcript of his talk and put the slides in the correct order.

First, I want to talk about shares that are mainly used to keep a tight rein on things. They are useful in that the more that you have, the more powerful you are. They don't suit everyone, only those with a strong interest in how things go for the company.

The next ones are really useful if some of your workforce want to leave the company. They can also be useful as an incentive for the members of the workforce, because they can be used as a reward for employees where dividends may be paid in addition to their salary.

After that, we have shares that mean you'll definitely get some sort of dividend, but it's not a fixed amount, and this type of share may vary, depending on the specific structure of the arrangement between the company and the shareholder.

The fourth type we have are where you're guaranteed a fixed dividend depending on the percentage stated in the preference share – and what you get really depends on how things go. You may get more of a dividend, or you may have more rights if things go really well. If you're investing in this type of shares, you need to look carefully at what's in it for the company and what's in it for you.

Finally, this class of share really depends on each individual situation, but it is really useful if two companies are entering a venture together. In this situation, the new shares created will give investors and shareholders protection, and the company documents may mean that a new director can be given these shareholdings. There are no hard-and-fast rules. It really depends on what's in the company Articles.

Thank you all for your patience; I hope I've been able to give you a rough outline in order for you to make an informed choice.

3 Read the transcript again and check any unfamiliar words. In pairs, take turns to choose a slide and describe the shares it illustrates in your own words without saying which slide you've chosen. Your partner must guess which one.

Listening

1 Discuss these questions with a partner.

1 How can a company borrow money to get it through a difficult financial period?
2 Explain the meaning of these terms.
- recession
- repayment
- lending institution
- share capital
- default
- charges
- securities

8 Company law 2

2 You are going to hear a conversation between a lawyer, Mark, and a corporate client, Helen.

a 🎧 30 **8.1** Listen to the first part of the conversation. Why is Helen contacting Mark?

b 🎧 31 **8.2** Listen to the second part and correct the incorrect statements.
1 Helen can make this decision herself.
2 Mark thinks raising share capital is the best option.
3 Helen should consider borrowing.
4 Marks thinks Helen has a strong company.
5 One answer might be to borrow from people within the company on an informal basis.

c 🎧 32 **8.3** Listen to the third part and complete this sentence.

A debenture sets out the (1)_____ of a loan, the (2)_____ borrowed, repayment (3)_____, charges (4)_____ the loan, (5)_____ for protecting and insuring the property, and terms for (6)_____ if the company (7)_____.

d 🎧 33 **8.4** Listen to the final part. What is Mark's final advice about charges?

Language work

3 a Complete the sentences below with the correct form of the phrasal verbs in the box.

get back	get through	go about	go for	go under	run by
	set out		take through		

1 Several companies have _____ _____ because of the recession this year, and others are on the verge.
2 Thanks for the advice. I'll _____ it _____ my colleagues at our next meeting.
3 We received a letter which _____ _____ all the relevant terms and conditions very clearly.
4 I'm sorry I couldn't _____ _____ to you yesterday, but we had a few problems with our email.
5 I'd be grateful if you could tell me how to _____ _____ buying shares in the company.
6 The lawyer _____ us _____ all the options before advising us on the most appropriate action to take.
7 The company's definitely strong enough to _____ _____ the next financial year.
8 Which type of shares are you going to _____ _____?

b Write four more gapped sentences using the phrasal verbs above for your partner to complete.

8 Company law 2

Reading 4

1 Read the informal email below from a businessman, Harry, to his lawyer, Jim, and choose the best answer – A, B or C – to these questions.

1 What does Harry want Jim to do?
   A Start proceedings to fight an insolvency action.
   B Give him some specific advice about his particular situation.
   C Advise him on how to manage his company's financial problems.
2 Where does Harry's company produce goods?
   A The Cayman Islands
   B Ireland
   C Another jurisdiction
3 Why does Harry think he can successfully fight the case?
   A Because he is protected by the law in the Cayman Islands.
   B Because his company doesn't operate in Ireland.
   C Because his company wasn't registered in Ireland.

To: Jim Swanson
From: Harry Matthews
Subject: Jurisdiction in insolvency

Dear Jim,

Just a very quick line to ask if you have any specific knowledge about the question of jurisdiction issues for insolvency proceedings. Unfortunately, things have gone really sour with the recession, and I'm afraid my company is having enormous financial problems. We're going to have a fight on our hands to keep it afloat.

I've been reading about Article 4 of EU Regulation 1346/2000. It has something in it that says that the law applicable to insolvency proceedings is that of the state where the insolvency proceedings were started. My situation is that my company is registered in the Cayman Islands, but the factory is in the middle of Ireland, and the whole workforce is from Ireland. However, all contact for orders, invoices and correspondence is through a shell office in the Cayman Islands. One UK creditor wants to commence insolvency proceedings in Ireland, but as far as I'm concerned, he's wasting his time. Should I let him just go ahead and then go to court and question the jurisdiction issue? What do you think? Can you just give me any thoughts you have on it?

I would really appreciate any help you can give me on this.

Talk soon.

Harry

---

2 Find phrases in the email that mean the following.

1 I'm writing briefly to …
2 we've had a bad time
3 It's going to need some hard work to …
4 in my opinion
5 do what he plans
6 I would be very grateful for …

8 Company law 2

3 Read these three extracts and answer the questions below.

Extract A

Commentary from an article on EU Insolvency Regulation 1346/2000
The Regulation applies to entities with a centre of main interests within the European Union only. The applicable court is the court where the debtors' centre of main interest is located. In most instances, this is where the registered offices of the company are, but this presumption can be rebutted. Whether insolvency proceedings are recognized will depend on the practices and legislation of each member state.

Extract B

In the case of *Re BRAC Rent-a-Car-International Inc.*, the company was incorporated in Delaware, but the company never traded in the United States, and all of its operations were conducted in England. This shows that the regulation may apply to entities even if they are incorporated outside the EU but have their centre of main interests in a member state. The judge took the view that limiting the effect of the regulation to entities incorporated within a member state would prevent it from achieving its purpose and leave it open to avoidance.

Extract C

An English case under the regulation initiated by a creditor and opposed by the company was Ci4net.com. The companies were registered in the United States and Jersey, but the creditor asserted that the centre of main interests was in England. The court identified the factor of the importance of creditors being certain in the knowledge of where they can pursue assets and that place having some element of permanence. The court was persuaded that correspondence and contact with their most substantial creditor all pointed to the companies having their principal executive offices in England, even though they were not registered there.

Which extracts talk about …
1 companies that the regulation is relevant to?
2 not restricting the extent of the regulation?
3 the usual definition of *centre of main interest*?
4 the importance of a company's clarifying where the main centre of interest is?

Language work

4 Find verbs in the extracts above which collocate with these words.

1 _____ a presumption
2 _____ insolvency proceedings
3 _____ operations
4 _____ a purpose
5 _____ / _____ a case
6 _____ assets

5 In pairs, discuss Harry's situation and decide what action Jim should recommend and why. You may find it helpful to highlight the relevant points in the three extracts above.

8 Company law 2

Writing

1 Write the email from Jim to Harry. Use expressions from the Useful language box where appropriate.

> **USEFUL LANGUAGE**
> As far as … is concerned, …
> As for … , / As regards … , / In relation to … , / In reference to … ,
> According to … ,
> My understanding of the commentary is that …
> In my opinion, you should … because …
> You have no choice but to …

2 Swap emails with your partner. Read his/her email, then write a reply, thanking him/her for the advice and saying what you're planning to do.

Speaking 1

1 a Look back at the situation in Listening, Exercise 2 (page 78). With a partner, role-play the conversation between Helen and Mark. Use the sentence starters in the Useful language box below.

b Imagine another situation where a lawyer is explaining options to a corporate client. Change partners and role-play the new situation.

> **USEFUL LANGUAGE**
> Let me …
> I know that …
> I'm not too sure that …
> I'd think about …
> Another thing you might consider is …
> In that case, it will mean …
> You know that I …
> I want to …
> I don't think that …
> Can you put …?
> Essentially what you're saying is …
> Will do, and …

2 On the next page are some questions that some law students asked their teacher about mergers and acquisitions.

a Discuss the questions with a partner.

b Match the questions (1–12) with the answers (a–l).

Questions

1. Is there any real difference between a merger and an acquisition?
2. When do we use the term *takeover*?
3. What constitutes a hostile takeover?
4. When is a takeover friendly?
5. How can smaller companies profit from being acquired by a larger company?
6. How can companies sometimes lose out after a merger?
7. Is it important for merging companies to be related?
8. What procedures need to be followed when one company is acquiring another?
9. Can you explain the meaning of *due diligence*?
10. What significance do warranties have in the context of mergers and acquisitions?
11. What are the potential benefits and drawbacks to shareholders when a merger takes place?
12. Is it possible to prevent a hostile takeover?

Answers

a. It is when the whole takeover process goes really smoothly. A public offer of stock or cash is made to a company, and the board of the target company publicly approves the terms of the buyout, even though the terms may be subject to shareholder or regulatory approval.

b. Yes. With the former, two companies combine to form a new company, whereas with the latter, a new company is formed by the purchase of one company by another.

c. There are many potential downsides for companies, including managers being over-involved in the big picture rather than paying attention to smaller, crucial details such as employer–employee relations; different corporate cultures, which are often overlooked when dealing with market synergies; and too much focus on integration and cost-cutting rather than on day-to-day business, which can result in loss of customer base.

d. Usually a smaller company does well from a merger with another company if it can add to the synergy between the two companies. For example, a small company may have an excellent distribution network but poor products, and another company has good products but an inefficient distribution set-up.

e. This term is used to describe an action where a company makes a bid for another company. If the shares of the company being targeted are quoted on the stock exchange, then an offer will be made for the outstanding shares.

f. Essentially, it is an investigation or audit of a potential investment. It can have other meanings in other legal contexts, but in the context of mergers and acquisitions, it can be carried out on the prospective assets and financial records of the targeted company.

g. This term is used when the takeover attempted is resisted by the company being targeted; the company does not approve of the buyout and fights the acquisition.

h. Usually, the first step is for the targeting company to start buying shares in the targeted company. If more than 5% of the shares are purchased, then the company must make a tender offer. The price offered is often at a premium compared to the market price, but acquisition of 5% or more of the shareholding must be disclosed to the relevant Securities & Exchange Commission. Once a tender offer is made, the targeted company may accept or negotiate or may use some hostile takeover defence, such as granting existing shareholders options to buy extra stock at a discount to reduce the acquiring company's share or find a 'white knight', such as a friendlier potential acquiring company. When a deal goes through, it can be a cash-for-stock transaction or stock-for-stock, and these can have different tax implications.

i No, though there should be some connection between them for some synergy to be beneficial.

j They may see the price of their shares rise or fall, depending on the success or otherwise of the newly formed company.

k Their importance is threefold. Together with representations from the seller, they enable the buyer to learn as much as possible about the seller and the business before the buyer signs the acquisition agreement. They are protective in that they give the buyer information to decide to walk away or renegotiate. They are supportive in that they give a framework for indemnification of the seller's obligations to the buyer after the closing of the deal.

l Yes, it is. Usually a company issues shares to its shareholders at a reduced price to try to retain control.

3 In pairs, choose one of the topics below. Prepare to talk about the topic for one minute. When your partner has finished his/her talk, ask a question about it.

Mergers and acquisitions
- Different types
- Risks
- Advantages
- Choosing a target company to acquire
- Procedures involved
- Possible problems

Language work

4 Complete this text about a merger using the words in the box.

| also | as | because | but | finally | in order | just |
| more importantly | | while | while | | | |

We'll take a look at One News and its acquisition of Allspace. (1)_____ you know, One News was one of the world's largest media conglomerates and Allspace was a social-networking site. Well, One News wanted to take advantage of internet advertising to move away from traditional advertising on TV and in newspapers, and Allspace had over 20 million users and an online advertising revenue model. (2)_____ there were many smaller social-networking sites competing with Allspace around 2005, One News made the right decision to acquire Allspace (3)_____ the site was quickly becoming the dominant player, not (4)_____ in the social-networking sphere, but in cyberspace in general. (5)_____ , the company had ample financial resources, IT expertise, server and hardware capacity, and operational knowledge and ability to ensure both the retention of existing users as well as capturing new users. (6)_____ One News used cross-selling methods, it was (7)_____ careful to ensure that Allspace executives had the freedom to allow the enterprise to thrive in its 'trendy' format. (8)_____ , Allspace not only continued to thrive under its own culture after the acquisition, (9)_____ the extra resources from a world-class conglomerate gave it additional resources (10)_____ to pursue further growth opportunities.

Research

5 Do some research on a recent merger that has made the headlines and write a short report about it using the linking words from Exercise 4.

Reading: Part 3

TIP
If you are unsure of the correct word, use your knowledge of typical endings to guess. Then read the whole text through; if your guess is incorrect, the right word may come to you as you see it in context.

Read this advice given on a Spanish website to company directors with insolvency problems. Use the words in the box to the left of each text to form one word that fits in the same numbered gap in the text.

0	DIRECT
1	PERSON
2	LAW
3	CONTRAVENE
4	OBLIGE
5	PROCEED
6	RISE

The law establishes a series of obligations for the (0) _directors_ and board members of such companies that, in the event that they are breached, consciously or unconsciously, the directors and board members will be held (1)_____ liable for the debts of the company. Among the most frequent causes of personal liability of a director are the following: undercapitalization (Section 104 of the Spanish Limited Liability Companies Act [LSRL] and Section 260 of the Spanish Public Limited Companies Act [LSA]), (2)_____ acts or acts in (3)_____ of the articles of association by the directors in prejudice of the interests of third parties (Section 133 of the Spanish Public Limited Companies Act) and in the event of being declared liable for the insolvency (Sections 164 and 165 of the Spanish Insolvency Act [LC]). Under these sections, probably the most frequent reason is for not complying with the (4)_____ laid down by the administrative body to petition for insolvency (5)_____ within the period of two months from when the situation of insolvency (6)_____ .

7	VOLUNTEER
8	OBJECT
9	SURVIVE
10	DETRIMENT
11	FURTHER
12	PRISON

In the event that (7)_____ insolvency proceedings are not started, the company is exposed to being subjected to obligatory insolvency proceedings by its creditors. The (8)_____ of these latter proceedings is not the (9)_____ of the company, but rather the suspension of its powers of administration and rights over its own assets, which are taken over by the receivers. This is (10)_____ to any endeavours to ensure that the companies continue trading and focuses more on settlement of its debts to creditors. (11)_____ , as we mentioned in the paragraph regarding directors' liability, a breach of the obligation to commence insolvency proceedings within a period of two months from the insolvency arising represents a breach of Sections 164 and 165 of the Spanish Insolvency Act which imposes sentences of (12)_____ from two to six years.

Speaking: Part 3

TIP
It is a good idea to turn to face your partner when doing this task, as it will encourage you to engage with the other person and not try to talk to the examiner.

A client owns a large electronics company. He is considering taking over a small company that supplies electronic components. Advise him on legal procedures and potential problems.

Discussion points
- What initial legal steps to take
- The risks involved
- The effect that a merger will have on the company structure

8 Company law 2

Listening: Part 1

TIP
Remember that the correct answer will not be in the same words in the recording as in the option, so you will need to listen to understand the general meaning.

You will hear three different extracts related to restructuring. For questions 1–6, choose the answer (A, B or C) which fits best, according to what you hear.

🎧 34 8.5 **Extract 1**
You will hear two lawyers talking about a colleague who is moving to the US.

1 Mike believes that lawyers in the US …
   A have an additional role to that of lawyers in the UK.
   B have to exert pressure on the companies to restructure.
   C do not have to work as hard as lawyers in the UK.

2 Restructuring in today's economic climate is not straightforward because …
   A different industries have different problems.
   B many problems require attention at the same time.
   C the traditional ways of dealing with restructuring are ineffective.

🎧 35 8.5 **Extract 2**
You will hear a lawyer talking to a colleague about the best people to consult about restructuring.

3 Why should companies not use their usual legal counsel when they want to restructure?
   A They cannot act very quickly.
   B Speed is not always the primary concern.
   C They don't have confidence in their experience.

4 Morris recommends using restructuring specialists because …
   A they have a great deal of court experience.
   B they are good strategists.
   C they are familiar with the relevant legal aspects.

🎧 36 8.5 **Extract 3**
You will hear a lawyer talking to a colleague about the success of his specialist restructuring firm.

5 What does James say about his restructuring firm today?
   A It has been expanding steadily for a long time.
   B There are a lot of rumours going round about the success of his firm.
   C It is doing much better now than it used to.

6 According to James, which law firms do best when it comes to finding credit?
   A Those that employ lawyers with accounting experience
   B Those that have dealt with financial institutions in the past
   C Those that have lawyers with the highest reputations

Writing: Part 2

TIP
Try to include examples to illustrate the different points you mention. You will often have to use language of speculation: For example, if partners don't … , they might find that …

A junior colleague is going to give a talk at a conference for young entrepreneurs about what can go wrong in a partnership and how to deal with this. He has asked for your suggestions on what to include. Write a memorandum to your colleague. Your memorandum should:

- explain why a strong business plan is vital
- point out the legal options when a partnership is failing
- outline the importance of a formal partnership agreement and clear exit strategy
- emphasize the value of legal advice when problems arise.

Write your answer in 200–250 words.

8 Company law 2

9 Environmental law

■ **Lead-in** Discuss these questions with a partner.

1 How important do you think it is for a lawyer to know about environmental law these days?
2 What types of problem might an environmental legal specialist have to deal with?
3 When might problems concerning environmental law cross jurisdictions?

Reading 1

1 You are considering doing a course on environmental law. Look at the two course outlines (A and B) below and on the opposite page and work with a partner to match these module titles (a–d) to the correct modules (1–4).

a Assessment, compliance and enforcement
b General aspects of international environmental law
c Environmental safeguarding
d Environmental democracy

A

Postgraduate Law Programme by distance learning
International Environmental Law

18 months' duration   Core modules 1 and 2 plus one elective

CORE MODULES
Module A1: (1) _____
Development and sources of international environmental law
Environmental governance, institutions and jurisdiction issues
Sustainable development

Module A2: Application and enforcement of international environmental law
Environmental damage and state responsibility
Civil liability for damage
Resolution of environmental disputes
Environment and human rights

ELECTIVES
Module A3: (2) _____
Marine environment protection
Conservation and biological diversity, principles and enforcement
Hazardous waste management and enforcement
Climate-change management and responsibility
or
Module A4: Transboundary environmental frameworks
Environment and trade
War and armed conflict – environmental considerations
Nuclear energy and environment
Cross-border pollution management and penalty enforcement

B

Postgraduate Masters of Laws LLM in EU Environmental Law by distance learning

18 months' duration *Core modules 1 and 2 plus one elective*

Core modules

Module B1: Environmental policies and principles of the EU
Shared responsibility, market-based instruments and holistic policy approaches
Principles of environmental policy (EC Art. 174(2),(3))
Rationale of the 'polluter pays' principle
Integrating environmental issues with economic policy
Aspects of the 'precautionary principle' (risk assessment and management)

Module B2: Making environmental law
Role of Council of Europe and European Parliament
Principle of attribution
Harmonizing legislation
Choice of legal basis for environmental laws

Electives

Module B3: (3) _____
Challenging the validity of EC legislation and decision-making (EC Art. 230)
Enforcement by the Commission
State responsibility for breaches by individuals and corporations
Penalties

or

Module B4: (4) _____
Rights to environmental information, participation and justice (the Aarhus Convention)
Human rights
Environmental rights embedded in national constitutions
European Convention of Human Rights

2 Which of the modules do you think would deal more specifically with each of these topics?

1 responsibility for causing / clearing up oil spills at sea
2 requirements on drilling for oil
3 drafting regulations prohibiting disposal of agricultural effluent into inland waterways
4 land zoning for growing bio-fuel constituents
5 environmental accountability for all nations
6 worldwide considerations for national legislators

Research

3 Choose two topics from the course outlines and research what might be covered in them. Write a short summary of each topic without using the words from the outlines. Swap with a partner and guess which topics the summaries relate to.

In this section of the module/elective, you will look at ...

Reading 2

1 On the next page, there are some blogs from a website for postgrad opportunities for law graduates. Read them and say which course from Reading 1 each person would choose.

2 Read the blogs again and answer these questions.

Which person/people (A, B, C, D or E):

1 thinks there might be some content overlap in certain sections of the course he/she would choose?
2 works in the public sector?
3 wants to change his/her specialization?
4 plans eventually to do both types of course?
5 would find it hard to choose an elective?
6 has been involved with an international organization?
7 is looking at the linguistic value of the course?

A — The International Environmental Law postgrad course would suit me better because I'm from Thailand and I intend to become a judge there some day. One of the qualifications I need is a Masters in Maritime Law, so a priority for me would be Modules 1 and 2, and I would do Module 3 as an elective. This would give me a start on these subjects. Moreover, as English is not my first language, by the same token it would be better for me to do this course and get to grips with the terminology before I go on to do the Masters Programme.
Daeng

B — Well, I am a tax lawyer practising in Germany, but I'm getting fed up with tax law and want to move into environmental law. Admittedly, the International Law Course looks very interesting, but on balance, I feel the EU course would be more suitable for me and my future career. Both score very highly for me on content, convenience and duration, but the overriding factor for me would be the relevance of the EU directives and their application within the EU, so I'd go for the EU one.
Bruno

C — Being from Brazil and having specialized in World Trade Organization Law, a big factor for me would be the elective in international law – the one dealing with environment and trade. Both are good from the convenience point of view, but on balance, I'd go for the international law one, as it would really be more relevant to what I need.
Uiara

D — I'm an in-house lawyer with a municipal city council in Austria, so for me, the EU one would be of the utmost importance. Both Modules 1 and 2 look really good as to content, but I'd have a bit of a struggle deciding on which elective to do. Both are highly relevant for what I do. On the one hand, I'd be interested in compliance and assessment for my job, but on the other hand, environmental democracy is so important. Admittedly, it would be more significant if I was working for an environmental non-governmental organization. It's a tough one, to pick one over the other, but I'd lean towards the environmental democracy elective, as Module 2 probably covers a lot of what's in Elective 3.
Aberie

E — I'm from Argentina and I feel that the environment is more of a global issue than being restricted to any one continent. International conventions have a huge impact, not only in the EU but all over the world. Therefore, a factor for me would be the subjects covered in Modules 1 and 2. I'm really interested in governance, as I worked on a committee for setting up an international environmental court on a par with the International Court of Human Rights. Admittedly, I'd be stuck trying to decide between the electives. However, if really pushed, I think that overall I'd have to go with Module 4 as an elective, as for me, it links nicely with Modules 1 and 2.
Adelmo

Language work

3 Complete these phrases that the blog writers use to express a preference.

1 It would _____ me better …
2 By the same _____ , …
3 On _____ , I feel …
4 Both _____ very highly for me …
5 The _____ factor for me would be …
6 A _____ factor for me …
7 From the convenience _____ of view, …
8 On the one _____ , I'd …
9 It's a _____ one.
10 I'd _____ towards …
11 A _____ for me would be …
12 If really _____ , …

4 Talk to your partner about a career decision/choice you will have to make soon. Use some of the phrases from Exercise 3.

Speaking

1 Work in small groups. You have been asked to give a training session on environmental law to lawyers in your country. Research one of the module topics in the courses and give a short talk on it.

2 Look at the course outlines in Reading 1 again (pages 86–87) and discuss with a partner which would you prefer to follow if you had to choose between them. Give your reasons.

> **USEFUL LANGUAGE**
>
> I'd much prefer to take the …
> I think the second course would be more beneficial.
> I think the first course would suit people who …
> The second course doesn't really cater for people who …
> In my opinion, a lot of sections of the first course wouldn't be relevant to …
> I'd far rather …
> The first course looks as though it goes into much more depth than …

Reading 3

1 Complete this opinion using words formed from those in brackets.

Federal Republic of Germany

In the present proceedings, the Commission is challenging the **(1)** _____ (*adequate*) of the transposition by Germany of Council Directive 90/313/EEC of 7 June 1990 on the freedom of access to information on the environment ('the Directive') on four points: the **(2)** _____ (*exclude*) of judicial bodies, the **(3)** _____ (*part*) supply of information, the scope of **(4)** _____ (*prelim*) investigation proceedings and the charging of costs.

The relevant legal provisions

The Directive is motivated by the **(5)** _____ (*presume*) set out in the third recital in the preamble that 'access to information on the environment held by public authorities will improve environmental protection'.

Its objective, as declared in Article 1, is 'to ensure freedom of access to, and **(6)** _____ (*disseminate*) of, information on the environment held by public authorities and to set out the basic terms and conditions on which such information should be made available'.

Article 2 defines the key terms 'information relating to the environment' and 'public authorities'.

Article 3 obliges Member States to ensure that their public authorities make available such information at the request of 'any natural or legal person … without his having to prove an interest'; it also permits **(7)** _____ (*refuse*) on specified grounds.

Article 4 stipulates a right of judicial or administrative review of decisions refusing access.

Article 5, which is **(8)** _____ (*centre*) to the most difficult issue in the present case, deals with the question of the charge which can be levied for supplying the information.

Article 6 extends the duties of public authorities under the Directive to 'bodies with public responsibilities for the environment and under the control of public authorities'.

Article 7 requires the Member States to publish **(9)** _____ (*period*) reports on the state of the environment. The remaining provisions of the Directive are not directly material in the present proceedings.

2 Read the complete opinion again and answer these questions.

1 Why does the Commission refer to Articles 1–7 of the Directive?
2 What is the Commission challenging?
3 What are the grounds of the challenge?

Language work

3 Change these words into the part of speech indicated.
1 assume (→ noun)
2 option (→ adjective)
3 finance (→ adjective)
4 conspire (→ noun)
5 realize (→ noun)
6 imagine (→ adjective)
7 deny (→ noun)
8 collude (→ noun)
9 history (→ adjective)

4 Find words in the opinion that mean the following.
1 adoption
2 range
3 conditions
4 introduction
5 involvement
6 specifies
7 imposed
8 relevant

5 a Use the correct form of words you found in Exercise 4 to complete these sentences.
1 The judge asked the lawyer if the witness's evidence was _____ to the case.
2 The _____ is quite long and complicated, but it's worth reading.
3 Do you think the government will _____ an additional tax on luxury goods next year?
4 People with a(n) _____ in the estate of H.J. Longman are asked to contact this office at the above address.
5 I'm afraid those matters are outside the _____ of this particular inquiry.

b Write five gapped sentences for a partner to complete using words from Exercises 1, 3 and 4.

6 a Read the opinion again. Your client is having problems understanding it. In pairs, rephrase it in more straightforward language.

b Change partners and role-play the conversation with your client. Use phrases from the Useful Language box.

> **USEFUL LANGUAGE**
> Sorry, I've got no idea what … means.
> Can you put this in language I can understand, please?
> Can you explain … ?
> This paragraph is unclear to me. Does it mean that … ?
>
> OK. To put it simply, it means …
> What it means is …
> Basically, it's saying that …

9 Environmental law

Reading 4

1 Read this senior partner's report on a current case and complete it using the words in the box.

affected	applied	concentration	criteria	drain	eliminating
interpretation		origin	protection		vulnerable

Polluter pays

The High Court has referred one of our cases to the European Court on the (1) _____ and validity of Directive 91/676 EC of 12th December 1991. The Court has referred the case for a decision on the 'polluter pays' principle.

Two issues came up during the case in relation to the application of the Directive. Firstly, community law cannot provide precise (2) _____ to establish in each case whether the discharge of nitrogen compounds of agricultural (3) _____ makes a significant contribution to the 'polluter pays' principle; and secondly, the Directive may be (4) _____ by the Member States in different ways.

The Article in question is Article 2(j) and 3(l) of 91/676. It concerns (5) _____ of waters against pollution caused by nitrates. Annexe 1 refers to identification of surface freshwaters as waters affected by pollution. (6) _____ zones are all known areas of land which (7) _____ into these waters and contribute to pollution. The Member State has an obligation to protect vulnerable lands. We believe, as a Member State, that the discharge of nitrogen compounds from agricultural sources makes a significant contribution to that overall (8) _____ of nitrates.

Our main argument is that if there is pollution already, then the Directive does not mean that farmers must take on the burden of (9) _____ pollution that they didn't contribute to. To put it another way, if the farmer didn't contribute, why should he pay for it, even though his land borders the waters (10) _____ ? We are arguing that the 'polluter pays' does reflect the principle of proportionality.

2 Read the report again and answer these questions in your own words.
1 On what grounds has the High Court referred the case?
2 What issue came up concerning the application of the Directive?
3 What does the Article in question concern?
4 What is the firm's main argument?

Listening

1 Discuss these questions with a partner.
1 Look at the toy. What sort of problems might it present regarding waste disposal and hazardous materials?
2 What do you know about the WEEE and RoHS Directives?

9 Environmental law

2 🎧 **37** **9.1** Listen to a conversation between a lawyer, Denise Howard, and her client, Martin James, who has a problem. Check your ideas from Exercise 1.

3 🎧 **37** **9.1** Listen again and make notes on the conversation under the following headings. If necessary, read the audio transcript on page 103.

Denis Sorter & Company Solicitors
Solicitor/ Client Attendance Form

DS

Name of client: _____

Reasons for meeting/telephone call: _____

Client's product details: _____

Initial problem: _____

Action already taken by client: _____

Client's current concern: _____

Matters discussed: _____
_____

Advice given: _____
_____

Activities agreed to be undertaken by the client: _____
_____

Activities agreed to be undertaken by lawyer: _____
_____

Writing

1 Imagine you are Denise Howard. Write up a report for your files from your notes on the conversation in Listening above. Use formal language and the passive where appropriate.

I informed him that …
I outlined …
I referred to …
I was contacted by Martin James on 2nd March.
Its heart lights up when it is hugged.

2 Summarize the conversation, giving the main points in an email to a colleague who is taking over your case load while you are on leave. Your language will be more informal here.

Hi David,
Thanks for taking over my cases for a few weeks. You may get a call from Martin James. I spoke to him last week about …

9 Environmental law

Reading: Part 4

Read this extract from an article about clinical legal education and the statements below. Choose the best sentences A–I to fill the gaps. There is one extra sentence which you do not need to use.

Clinical legal education and environmental law

Moot courts and simulations provide training in written and oral advocacy for law students and are becoming a popular feature of Clinical Legal Education Programmes worldwide. **(1)** _____ This reduces the opportunities for students to engage with the practical application of legal theory to real-life scenarios. **(2)** _____ Students may have opportunities to engage in diverse and practical activities such as drafting legislation and negotiating simple or complex matters.

Clinics are conducted within the university learning framework, offering a model of learning by doing, and often have extensions into the wider community, with students engaging in pro-bono work within the community. **(3)** _____ The teaching and learning of environmental law lends itself well to the methodology of clinical legal education, where students can collaborate, feedback, critique, review and intervene. **(4)** _____

An example of such a simulation is one used by the Stanford Law School, which centres around the use of a fumigant in the strawberry fields in California. **(5)** _____ Students are assigned to be either the legal, scientific or community representatives of the residents or the staff of the administrative agency involved in the issue of permits. **(6)** _____ The simulation trains students to acquire the basic skills to undertake research, writing and presentation of scientific and legal information and arguments to both lay and regulatory audiences. Furthermore, students learn how to determine and understand the underlying causes of scientific debate surrounding the use of fumigants within a legal framework.

(7) _____ This provides students with opportunities for training in basic interviewing and counselling skills, and how to deal with the differing and sometimes conflicting perspectives of the public, scientists and legal professionals. A simulation involving a property developer presents students with opportunities to look at and present arguments from both economic and environmental perspectives.

Simulations and case studies are of invaluable assistance to students in bridging the gap between theory and real-life situations. **(8)** _____ They allow for controlled and scalable interventions by the academic teaching team and can be maximized by cross-disciplinary co-operation, for example by collaboration between course designers or lecturers on a human-rights course a trade-law course and an environmental law course.

> **TIP**
> Remember that to fit the gap, the sentence must relate directly to the context *and* fit grammatically. Read the whole text before trying to fit the options and be aware that some options may be quite similar, but only one fits exactly.

A Supervision of students in this context is of critical importance from the perspective of the student, university and the community.

B They can also be useful in providing professors with well-defined learning objects.

C At the same time, they can be taught, monitored and inspired.

D Case studies which form a basis for simulations can provide an efficient and effective methodology which incorporates and integrates doctrinal learning and theory with skills.

E Another simulation concerns the health complaints of a fictional farmer and his family working in cotton fields.

F They have to prepare briefs and present oral testimony and arguments before an administrative officer in support of their respective positions.

G If properly constructed, they can be a rewarding experience for students.

H It features an appeal by residents living near the strawberry fields against the granting of a permit to allow such use.

I The development of clinical legal education stems from an awareness of the heavy reliance of most law courses on the analysis of theoretical frameworks underlying the practice of law.

Speaking: Part 3

> **TIP**
> The discussion points are there to help you, but if you don't use them, you won't be penalised. Remember, this is a joint task, and you can always ask your partner to add, help, clarify, etc. as you would in a normal conversation/discussion.

TASK
Your client wants to build a new runway at a small provincial airport, but has not yet received planning permission. Advise him on what he should consider.
Here are some discussion points to help you.

- The importance of making an environmental impact assessment
- Why and how he should keep the public informed of the plans
- The legal steps to take if there is opposition

9 Environmental law

Listening: Part 3

TIP
Before you listen for the first time, read through the options and questions and underline key words so you know what you are listening for – *person/reason/times*, etc. If you can't decide which option to choose, use a process of elimination.

🎧 **38** **9.2** You will hear part of a conversation between a lawyer, Mrs Clarke, and her client, Mr Davies. It concerns an environmental problem. For questions 1–5, choose the best answer (A, B or C).

1 Who is Mr Davies?
   A A farmer
   B Another lawyer
   C An environmentalist

2 What is he concerned about?
   A There are not sufficient waste-disposal facilities in the area.
   B Increased industrial development is encroaching on the farmers' land.
   C The land has become contaminated.

3 Mr Davies believes that the farmers have a case because …
   A decisions were made without proper consultation.
   B not enough initial research was done.
   C access to their land should not be restricted.

4 Mrs Clarke advises that the 'polluter pays' principle …
   A must be complied with.
   B cannot be used for direct legal action.
   C is based on community environmental policy.

5 Why are dates important in Mrs Clarke's opinion?
   A To calculate the extent of the damage
   B To comply with the Environmental Liability Directive
   C To document previous legal action

Writing: Part 1

TIP
When you have finished your letter, check for accuracy, appropriacy, organization and range of vocabulary. Consider whether the reader would be fully informed.

You are a lawyer and you are representing a group of residents who are opposed to the extension of Grantham Port by the Grantham Port Authorities on land adjacent to their properties.
Mr Marcus from the Port Authorities has written to Mrs Kindle, the head of the residents' opposition group. Read the letter, on which you have made some notes. Then, using all the information in your notes, write a letter to Mr Marcus, on behalf of the residents.

Thank you for your letter concerning the planned port extension in Hebdon Bay.
We appreciate the concern of local residents, but must point out the need for such an extension to cope with increased port activity in the coming years.

[note: no – noise, traffic – point out]

During the construction of the port, we assure you that there will be very little disruption to daily life in the area and when complete, there will be minimal impact on the lives of those living nearby.

[note: huge impact, infrastructure unable to cope – describe]

[note: why no public meetings?]

In all stages of the planning process, we have followed proper procedure, including full environmental impact assessments. All information is available for the public to read on our website.

[note: EIA incomplete – request further details to be made available]

We hope that the benefits this port extension will bring by utilizing an area of hitherto unused ground will be recognized by the public.

[note: many protected species here – explain]

Yours sincerely
Jack Marcus
Grantham Port Authorities

9 Environmental law

Audio transcripts

Audio 1.1

Mr Howard: Good morning, Professor Daykin. It's good to talk to you again. What can I do for you?

Professor Daykin: It's good of you to speak to me – I know you're a very busy man. This is just so difficult. I really don't know what to do. I've been working at Sarvat for the past twenty years and nothing like this has ever happened to me before. I mean, I just can't believe it. A place with such a high reputation – to let this happen – and now I have to contact you. I've only ever had to contact a lawyer once before in my life, and that was when I was buying my house. Ages ago. We've known each other from the tennis club for years, but I never thought I'd see the day when I'd have to contact you in a professional capacity. I've got no alternative. I've been thinking about this all week, and it's affecting me badly.

MH: You're clearly very upset, Professor. Would you like to make an appointment and come in and have a chat when you're feeling a bit better?

PD: No, no, no, I don't want to make it that formal yet, if that's all right. I really need to just talk it through at this stage. I mean, maybe it's nothing, maybe nothing can be done. I feel so angry. I mean, how could they do this to me?

MH: You know, sometimes it's good to write it all down and maybe send it in to me, so that I can have a better look at what you've written and get back to you, rather than doing this on the phone.

PD: No, I'll try and give you a quick outline, and you can let me know what you think. Is that all right?

MH: Fine. You go ahead, and I'll make some notes.

PD: Thank you so much. It's like this … you see, I have an arrangement with Sarvat University Press. In fact, most of the professors here have this arrangement. We select the contents of course packs. They usually consist of journal articles, newspaper articles, course notes or syllabi, sample test questions, excerpts from books … that sort of thing. We deliver the contents to the copy shop with an estimate of the number of students on the course. The materials are assigned to the students, so the copy shop knows who is eligible to buy the packs if they want to. I must emphasize that these packs are designed solely for the students on a particular course. Any course packs that are not bought by the students are usually destroyed by the copy shop. However, what happened was that the copy shop made multiple copies of the materials which we provided and then sold them on to other students for a profit.

MH: Who looks after copyright payments and permission for the professors?

PD: It's Sarvat University Press. They have a department that receives and processes requests for permission to use any copyrighted works. They usually charge a fee and generally share these fees with the authors.

MH: So, who is affected by this?

PD: Well, a lot of the material in question belongs to some of my very close friends in the academic world, who I have the greatest respect for. Their trust in me has been badly affected by all of this. The course packs were prepared for selling commercially in a limited capacity. The copyrighted works are valuable original works. I mean, surely copyright protection is supposed to protect authors, and only those who pay can copy excerpts of copyrighted works for a variety of purposes?

MH: I feel at this stage that you should write out in detail what you've told me and send it to me so that I can look into the matter further and get back to you. I have the gist of it, but I would need to look at it much more carefully. I can certainly understand how you feel. The quicker we deal with it the better.

PD: That's excellent. I'll get down to it right now, and maybe you could give me a call when you've had a chance to look at it.

MH: That sounds perfect. Now, if you'll excuse me, we'll have to leave it at that for now. I'll be in touch as soon as possible, Professor. Goodbye for now.

PD: Thank you very much for your time, Mr Howard. I feel better already. Goodbye.

Audio 1.2

Before the break, we were talking about copyright, and I'd like to continue by looking at some of the industries that are more likely to have their designs copied than others. Near the top of this list is the fashion industry. Everyone knows that haute-couture designs are regularly copied and sold cheaply on the high street, and the fashion houses really need to take more action to protect their new collections.

The problem is getting worse. Copyists today are faster and better than ever before. As soon as a model moves onto the catwalk, the design is being drawn by someone in the audience, and within weeks (sometimes even after a few days) we can buy the cheap copy on the high street. Fashion magazines even tell us where to find them!

So why is this allowed to continue? Why don't the high-profile designers take action against such obvious infringement of copyright law? Well, there are a couple of reasons. One is that up until now, copying has been considered almost an inevitable part of the business – it's something that has always happened and always will, whatever the big designers try to do about it. Another reason is that many designers consider imitation to be a form of flattery – only the good designs are copied. It's almost like an advertisement for the fashion house!

But neither of these reasons should prevent fashion houses from taking the relevant action, and it's time that they took steps to protect their innovations. Like other industries, they need to challenge the copyists, not accept them. At long last, it seems that this is beginning to happen. There are a couple of high-profile cases we can look at. Last year, the French fashion house Chloe took action against Top Shop, and the high-street shop had to stop selling a particular item and pay substantial damages. Another famous name, Jimmy Choo, forced Marks and Spencer to withdraw a £9.50 handbag that was a copy of a Jimmy Choo one that sells for £495. Yet another chain, New Look, had to pay them compensation for copying a shoe design. Although the details are not known, the amount is said to have been significant.

It is still rare for these cases to reach court, as most parties prefer to settle without admitting liability. But at least it shows that designers and retailers are becoming more aware and active. And what they really need to do is to protect their designs well before they show them to the public. Many designers think that it is unnecessary to register their designs at any stage because they are covered by copyright laws – from the first drawings.

Unfortunately, this deterrent is unlikely to be enough to stop imitations appearing on the high street. Designers really need to register protection before the clothes appear on the catwalk. Doing this is quite straightforward and inexpensive. It is also wide ranging. Registered Design Protection can cover all aspects of design, from shape to pattern. And it's not limited to clothes. It can protect accessories such as jewellery, bags and belts, too. Designers cannot apply for Registered Design Protection after the designs have become public, so they need to think about this at an early stage. To look at Registered Design Protection in more detail, we need to consider …

Audio 2.1

Andrew: Janet, while I'm away, I'm handing over my cases to Sylvia. But I'd like to run through a couple of them with you so you've got the background too, just in case she has any problems.
Janet: Good thinking. Have you filled in a legal elements chart for her? It usually makes things a lot clearer.
A: Yeah. Here it is. It's mostly complete. I just need to fill in a few more facts and figures.
J: OK.
A: Right. Our client is Jupiter Electronics, a small retail chain – they've been in business for twenty years. They sell radios, televisions, refrigerators and household appliances. Baker Retail is a chain of department stores. Appliance Zone is a national manufacturer, and Cool Places are their distributor. Jupiter Electronics is suing all of them. They're saying that Baker Retail and the manufacturers and distributor conspired among themselves either not to sell to our client or to do so only at discriminatory prices and highly unfavourable terms. Apparently, they told Jupiter earlier this year that they would sell TVs to him at twenty per cent *over* the price they were selling to other distributors, and they offered him refrigerators at forty per cent over the cost to others … and they justified it on the basis that his chain is open twenty-four hours and that therefore he could sell the goods on at a higher price!
A: But fixing the prices at twenty and forty per cent over the cost to others is in breach of Sections 1 and 2 of the Sherman Act.
J: Yep, absolutely. Section 1 of Sherman makes any contract or conspiracy illegal if it's in restraint of trade, and Section 2 forbids monopolization of interstate commerce. Um, OK, more details. Our client's manager, James Hull, phoned the manufacturers, Appliance Zone, three times in the week of the twenty-fifth of May and spoke to the managing director, asking him to reconsider the position. Mr Hull also called Cool Places five times in the week of the twenty-ninth of June for the same reason.
A: So, what are Baker Retail, Appliance Zone and Cool Places saying?
J: Well, their defence is that there are hundreds of other retailers selling the same and competing appliances in the same community. They are going to contend that the controversy is purely a private quarrel between our client and the chain of department stores, and that this does not amount to a 'public wrong' as is proscribed by the Sherman Act.
A: A private quarrel! That's ridiculous.
J: Exactly! The volume of the correspondence shows a lot more than a private quarrel. There are letters going back over five years on this. And the number of letters and the tone and the language used reinforce this. I mean, one letter states that our client 'is such a small merchant and his business is so small that if his business goes under, it will have no effect on the economy, and therefore the Competition Acts don't apply to him'!
A: Well, I suppose that's one argument!
J: I suppose so! In addition to this, they all deny that they refused to supply Jupiter with the Zoony range. Um, as you know, this range is really big, and they sell it to other outlets in the community, but Jupiter says that they won't sell or supply to them. Jupiter has written about ten times asking them for terms and supplies of certain three-eight-oh models of TVs. The defence's lawyers are arguing that the public is not affected by all this, but we need to show that this *is* a type of public harm. The defendant has no defence, and this is a clear attempt to monopolize.
A: Well, the facts as you present them seem to point towards a conspiracy in restraint of trade, a combination of monopolizing or trying to monopolize interstate commerce, the creation of a monopoly and public harm, all forbidden by the Sherman Act.
J: Yes – I think our client has quite a good case, really.

Audio 2.2

A: Shall I fill in some more of the facts and figures for Sylvia on the chart?
J: That would be great. Thanks.
A: OK. First – you said that Baker Retail told Jupiter early last year that they would sell at twenty per cent over. When exactly was that?
J: It was in early January.
A: And when did you say James Hull phoned them three times?
J: That was in the week of the twenty-fifth of May. He then called Cool Places five times in the week of the twenty-ninth of June.
A: Sorry, what was that last date?
J: The week of the twenty-ninth of June.
A: Great. And you mentioned something about him being a small merchant and Competition Laws not applying to him. When was that?
J: Er, the relevant letters were dated the twelfth, seventeenth and twenty-eighth of December.
A: Did you say seventh or seventeenth?
J: Seventeenth. Oh, and, um, note down, too, that he contacted them about the Zoony range about ten times. About selling three-eight-oh models of TVs.
A: Could you just give me that again?
J: Er, yep – the models were three-eight-ohs, and he contacted them at least ten times. Sylvia can get the exact dates from the files.
A: That's fine, really clear! You can go off on your break with no worries!

Audio 2.3

Extract 1

A: Hi! Are you going on this five-day summer school on competition law?
B: You mean the one at Exeter in August?
A: Yeah. It sounds excellent.
B: I wish I could, but I've got far too much on at the moment, and the firm's cutting down on extra training this year. Mind you, I did go to a fair number of courses last year. It's a shame, though. I think this one is going to be really good. Are you going?
A: Yeah. I'm particularly interested in the non-EU and US comparisons and also getting updated on the latest reforms. There's a good session on managing the relationship with the competition authorities. The boss wants me to report back on that one.
B: I'd appreciate some notes on that, too, if you wouldn't mind.
A: Not at all. I obviously can't go to all the sessions, but I'm going to make a point of getting to all the practical ones – the workshops and case studies. I really enjoy them. I get a bit bored with formal presentations all the time.
B: Too right! What I like about these events is the opportunity to network with people from different countries and different backgrounds. It can be very useful. Have a great week!

Extract 2

A: I hear that the OFT are investigating Tesco and Asda again for price fixing. The big supermarkets are really coming under fire at the moment!
B: Yeah. I think the OFT are going a bit far this time, though. It's a real fishing trip. They don't have real cause – I mean, look at the information they're asking for – it's so wide ranging – they're just hoping to get lucky!

A: I know what you mean. Only last week, the OFT had to apologize to Morrison's. Remember they claimed they were pushing up prices of dairy products back in 2003? Well, now they've had to admit they were wrong. They've got to pay them a hundred thousand pounds, too.

B: Yeah. I know the big supermarkets have to be kept in check, otherwise we'll all suffer, but sometimes I think the OFT are just abusing the power they've got. This latest inquiry will go nowhere.

Extract 3 8

A: So, you studied in Oxford for a while. Why go there instead of studying in Paris?

B: Oh, it wasn't instead of studying in Paris – it was as well as! I combined my PhD in Competition law in Paris with the LLM programme in Oxford.

A: What made you do that?

B: Well, I chose this particular Oxford college because of its ranking and its ongoing involvement in the field of competition law. And also because it offers a choice of different competition-law courses which I couldn't find anywhere else.

A: I've been wondering about continuing my legal studies in England, too. Your English has improved so much since you went there – a good knowledge of English has got to be an advantage in our profession.

B: Absolutely. And I can really recommend this college. They run an excellent International and Comparative Competition Law course, and I know you're interested in that. Personally speaking, doing that course has been so good for my career – not only academically, but it's also opened the doors of so many international law firms for me.

Audio 3.1 9

Peter: Hi, John. This is Hannah. We were at college together a couple of years back. She's left the legal profession already to follow a career exclusively in mediation.

Hannah: Hi, John. Nice to meet you. Peter tells me that you specialize in employment law like he does.

John: Yeah, that's right. I've been working in employment law now for going on eighteen months, but it seems a lifetime! So, you left the law for mediation. How's that going for you?

H: I'm really enjoying it!

J: What's your area? Or don't mediators have to specialize?

H: Yeah, I specialize in workplace and employment mediation.

J: So, can I ask you, what exactly does a mediator do?

H: Well, the important thing about a mediator is that he or she is neutral. We must be completely independent, with no vested interest in the outcome. What we do is maintain the momentum towards a solution so that as each side adopts a more positive view, resolution becomes the common aim of the parties. We never impose a settlement. We're only interested in helping the parties reach a mutually acceptable solution.

J: Mm. But you must have had to learn some really special skills to do this. It can't be easy! There was a case I had recently, and the thought of going into the same room with my client – who was an absolute tyrant – and her boss – who was the most ignorant and rude person you have ever met – would fill me with horror! It was hard enough for the judge to deal with the two of them, because they were at each other's throats, even during the evidence. The boss kept on interrupting my client when she was giving evidence.

H: So how did the judge deal with it?

J: Well, at one stage, he had to threaten the boss with imprisonment for contempt of court if he didn't keep quiet. That did it, and he shut up. But the atmosphere between them was awful, and when the judge ordered that my client be reinstated in her job, I couldn't help thinking that things had got so bad that the two of them would never be able to work together again. And sure enough, I got a letter from her a month later saying that although she'd won her job back, she couldn't stand working there any more and she'd moved to a new job.

H: A classic case for mediation! A basic part of our training is to create a safe environment. In this safe environment, each party can identify and acknowledge each other's needs and interests. This means we can broaden the search for options, make informed decisions and then the parties can move towards improved relationships. The mediator's job is to support both parties and to reduce tension and anxiety. It's vital for the parties to talk honestly and frankly about what happened and how it affected them. Then we have to find a way to use this information to clarify the problem and to identify a path to resolution.

P: Really! That's almost the complete opposite to what lawyers do!

H: Well, it definitely takes practice and a lot of self-control, and you really have to be able to read people.

J: It sounds really interesting and satisfying as a job – it doesn't seem to just focus on winning a case, but winning for both parties to be able to work together. Maybe I should consider a career move as well.

Audio 3.2 10

A: Good afternoon, Mr Franks. It's good to see you again. I understand you have some questions about monitoring your employees in the workplace?

B: Yes. I'm not particularly worried about any specific individual, I just have a few general questions if that's OK?

A: Of course. I hope I can help. So, what are your general concerns?

B: Well, I think everyone these days is aware of the dangers that the internet can bring into the office – I'm not talking about viruses and things like that, but how it can be misused and abused by people.

A: Are you thinking in terms of employees wasting time logging onto social networking sites when they should be working or using the phone for personal matters … ?

B: Well, that's one concern, obviously, but it's not only that. I hear that employers can actually be held liable for what their employees do online. Is that right?

A: Mm-hm. It is possible. There have many instances of claims for sexual harassment because bad jokes or photographs have been circulated by email – and a court has now decided that the employers could be liable for this, because it's happening on their networks.

B: That's worrying!

A: There is also the possibility that employers could be liable for defamatory statements made online.

B: Ah, I hadn't considered that.

A: And did you know that figures show that 84% of serious frauds are committed by employees – and a large number of these through using the internet? So, breaches of security and confidentiality are also important to consider.

B: So, what can I, as an employer, do about controlling my employees' use of the internet and phones? I don't imagine I'm legally entitled to install CCTV to watch their every move!

A: No, you're not. Employees have the right to a reasonable amount of privacy in the workplace. The laws governing use of CCTV are quite complex. Also, it would show a complete lack of trust in your staff, and I'm sure you don't want that.

B: No, of course not. But what *can* I do? I know that phone calls can be recorded 'for training purposes' as long as the parties involved know about it and there are itemized phone records that show who has phoned which numbers. But apart from that, is there anything else that isn't against the law?

A: Well, I think the best way forward is to develop a company policy on use of the internet and phones. And you must print

this out and inform your staff. Put up notices if you like, so that everyone knows what is expected. Also, you must set out clearly what disciplinary measures you will take if they fail to comply. Then everyone knows where they stand.
B: And if I suspect that someone is failing to comply?
A: Mm, it depends how serious it is. In certain cases, interception of email and CCTV monitoring is a possibility. But you don't want to go down that route unless you absolutely have to.
B: I see what you mean, but I need to have …

Audio 4.1

So, essentially, when you're drafting a contract, you have to make sure that the contract establishes agreement, rights, obligations and remedies. You also have to plan ahead in the contract for problems like termination and also how the contract is going to be interpreted. You must also pay attention to clauses that address the possibility of future litigation, like ADR clauses. Now, there are a few clauses that I want to mention specifically. These aren't frequently emphasized in general contract law, but they really are important for the purposes of drafting a contract. First, the integration clause, or, as it is also known, the entire agreement clause. The purpose of this clause is to state that there are no representations, warranties, terms or conditions between the parties other than those set out in the agreement. They prevent related dealings or previous agreements between the parties being used to vary or interpret the provisions of the contract. Next, we have the waiver clause. This deals with situations if parties want to waive a breach or default of a provision of the agreement. Then there's the 'time of the essence' clause, which is self-explanatory, and the survival clause, where parties might want duties and obligations to survive after the termination of the contract. The severability clause is also important, because if the contract is ever litigated, it's possible that a court might only strike down a part of a contract. So there can be agreement in a contract that the invalid illegal or unenforceable bit can be severed so that the rest of the agreement can continue to have effect.

Audio 4.2

Now, some general drafting rules. Avoid legal pairs and phrases like *at or about*, *any or all*, *basic and fundamental*, *full and complete*. Make the language simple. This is especially important in international contracts. So instead of *perform*, use *do*; for *render*, use *make*, *give* or *give back*. For *commence*, use *begin* or *start*. For *terminate*, use *end* or *stop*. I have a handout listing some common contract words and their simplified versions, which you can have at the end of the lecture, so enough about them. Next point: use active sentences rather than passive ones, and for heaven's sake keep sentences short. One fifty-word sentence can be made into three short sentences. If you make the sentence too long, you may contradict yourself, and this would be disastrous in a contract. Keep subjects and verbs together, keep compound verbs together and put verbs early.

Audio 4.3

Reconcile yourself to having to write many, many drafts of the contract to get it right. If you try to get all the details right in the first draft, you're likely to miss some larger points. Let the first draft be creative, thorough and imperfect. Use simple, clear, businesslike language. Use technical terms only when you have to. Make each clause do only one thing. Outlines can help you here by breaking the whole contract down into a series of small parts. When revising, check for ambiguities, like referring to the same person, item or concept by two different terms, as it creates ambiguity that can lead to misunderstandings later. After polishing each clause, read the document as a whole, as you may fix a problem in a clause, but cause more problems for the whole contract. Consult others, as two heads are often better than one. And finally, revising. Don't revise as you write. It slows down the writing and the revising process. Concentrate on your ideas when you write and revise later. Check for accuracy, organization, readability and style. Now, in the next lecture, I will focus on some examples, so I'm giving you them as handouts. Please have a look at them and bring them to the lecture tomorrow. That's all for now. Thanks.

Audio 4.4

Speaker 1

A lot of people think that by using standard English when drafting contracts, it is in fact over-simplifying things and losing the professional touch. And people confuse using accessible language with simplifying the content of the contract, too. This is definitely *not* what it's all about. The complexity of a contract depends on the underlying issues, and this won't change; but what *can* change is using language that isn't clear, and that can prevent anyone – that is, the average businessman like me or even lawyers themselves – from understanding what the contract says. Using standard English is simply using language that a normal, educated person can read and understand. Nothing more than that!

Speaker 2

I know I'm pretty new to this, but what really gets me is the completely ridiculous language that you sometimes see in contracts – you know, like *witnesseth*! There are so many archaic words lawyers have used in contracts for centuries that really shouldn't have a place in modern-day contracts. But words like that, although they may be irritating to people like me, don't actually cause any real problems. What is dangerous and needs to be looked at is the use of phrases like *hold harmless* which don't actually have a clear meaning and can be interpreted by clever lawyers to mean what is best for their client! Change has got to come soon, and it's probably going to be from the newer members of the profession like me.

Speaker 3

There's something that I always remind my junior partners of when they're drafting a new contract and that is – ideally – they should be able to justify the choice of each word in a contract. We lawyers often use standard fixtures when drafting, but we shouldn't always assume they are appropriate for all contracts. Obviously, I'm thinking of a best-case scenario – realistically, there isn't enough time to check every provision – but over a period of time, lawyers should build up a bank of provisions they have thoroughly scrutinized and learn to question the language more.

Speaker 4

We've been studying the language of contracts recently, and it's actually quite interesting. Apparently, people in the legal profession often tend to assume that vagueness and ambiguity are one and the same thing, but in fact there's a significant difference. Ambiguity can be dangerous, in that any ambiguous word or term can lead to different interpretations and therefore be a source of dispute. Vagueness, on the other hand, is more simply a lack of precision, often employed by lawyers who are unsure about future circumstances and wish to allow for several possibilities. Wherever possible, it's always better to be precise when drafting a contract to eliminate any misunderstandings.

Speaker 5

Traditionally, lawyers have spent a great deal of time focusing on the language of contracts. As I tell my students, today's technology is making this a much easier and less time-consuming process, with more and more companies using automated contract drafting. This releases the lawyer to spend more time focusing on what is really important – the negotiating side of things. This is really where a lawyer comes into his own and where the big decisions are made. However, technology should not be allowed to take control – and lawyers must be aware of the pitfalls as well as the advantages!

Audio 5.1

Pavla: Stefan, I missed the second part of the lecture on damages. Could you go through it with me?

Stefan: No problem, Pavla – it's quite straightforward. It was just clarifying the different types of damages. Firstly, the lecturer talked about liquidated damages, which you get when the contract states a fixed amount of damages in case of a breach. These are also called 'stipulated damages'. This means that if anything goes wrong, then the amount stated is all that the parties can get. OK so far?

P: Yep. Got that.

S: OK. He went on to talk about special damages. This is when the damages can be vouched.

P: You've lost me. 'Vouched'?

S: That's when they can be proved in court. I imagine the party would need receipts to be able to prove the expense.

P: OK. I get you.

S: Then there's reliance damages, where the injured party has to show that they had suffered a loss by relying on the contract and that this needs to be compensated. OK?

P: Right. Is that it?

S: Nearly there! He also talked about consequential damages. In some jurisdictions, it's the same thing as special damages, but basically they relate more to the type of breach and don't have such limited vouching restrictions.

P: Sounds a bit confusing!

S: Mm, you bet! And then there's specific performance. This is essentially where the court orders the breaching party to complete the contract. It's a common-law remedy available in equity, so the rules of equity apply. It's a type of injunction where the court orders something to be completed.

P: And equity is …?

S: Right. Equity is a special branch of common law where certain conditions have to be fulfilled before the remedy can be given, but that's another story!

Audio 5.2

Good morning, ladies and gentlemen. Welcome to this conference on Contract and Commercial Law. First of all, I'd like to introduce myself. I'm a contract and commercial lawyer and a managing partner with Fried, Sonner and Wall. We're all aware of how important it is to keep up to date with developments and trends in contract and commercial law, to ensure that we do not expose ourselves, our law firms or our clients to unnecessary risk. We're also particularly aware of the difficulty involved in finding the time to attend events like this. For that reason, we have specifically designed this very concise and practical seminar for the busy in-house and private-practice lawyers. We aim to provide up-to-the-minute and practical advice on the latest developments in contract law in just one intensive day.

Our unique programme covers the most important areas of contract law. All the speakers are experts in their fields and have extensive practical experience within the key areas covered in the seminar. They'll be available to answer your questions throughout the day. My task here is to give you a brief overview of the course. We'll be starting with developments in contract law covering several areas. These include: pre-contract agreements, offer and acceptance, duty of care, best and reasonable endeavours and, of course, the jurisdictional issue. By the end of the course, you will be in a position to master the effective negotiating and drafting of IT contracts in view of the recent developments in this area. We shall also be looking at the famous $2m Comma case, which some of you may be familiar with. We are lucky enough to have the successful lawyer who was involved in the case here with us today in Munich. He'll give us an insight into the importance of punctuation in contract clauses, as well, of course, as other matters.

Another topic of today's seminar will be how to deal effectively with damages to avoid unnecessary and sometimes costly disputes. Here, we'll be looking in depth at consequential loss and liquidated damages and we'll be covering the latest developments in damages for breach of contract, penalties and, of course, the latest case law on all of these areas.

Let me briefly outline the rest of the areas we're going to cover. 'Drafting guarantee indemnities' – which, as we all know, is crucial for the contract and commercial lawyer – is one topic. Another will be how best to exclude and limit contractual liabilities for your organization. Many of the leading players in the area of resolving commercial disputes are with us today, and they'll be sharing their knowledge and expertise and giving us valuable tips and techniques. I'm sure you'll find this an interesting, exciting day of seminars. So, now I'll hand over to our first speaker, who will knowledgeably take you through the intricacies of drafting and negotiating the IT contract. May I introduce Mr Frans Viedrict, senior partner in …

Audio 6.1

Mr Hockney: Good morning, Mrs Grant. It's good to speak to you. How can I help?

Mrs Grant: Well, as you know, I've been in the IT business for a long time, but what I'm really interested in is going out on my own. I want to branch into supplying computer parts and accessories, and I've been looking around for a commercial premises. I've found an ideal location, with good parking for customers, which would also be big enough for my son to set up his own business in the same premises as well. He's followed a different path from me and he wants to open an animal-accessories shop! I know the two don't exactly go hand in hand, but the frontage of the building is really big, with two separate entrances, so it can be done. So, first of all, I need some preliminary advice from you, and then hopefully you'll be able to negotiate commercial leases for both me and my son.

MH: Sounds an interesting venture! Well, I'm sure I can help. There are a number of things which I'll need, and if you have the information, fine. If not, I can get it from the agent. Do you have his details?

MG: Yes, I'll email them to you when we come off the phone.

MH: Great. OK, now, before I go near negotiating, I need you to think about a number of points and then come back to me. Firstly, in a commercial lease, you'll have to pay a security deposit before you move in, so you need to work out how much you can afford and likewise your son.

MG: Will I get it back when I move in?

MH: That depends. Some landlords keep part of it as security against any damage to the property. So you need to decide how much you can pay and how much you need to get back.

MG: Understood.

MH: Now, we also need to consider how the utilities are going to be paid – whether they will be shared between you and you son and whether you will both pay them directly to the service provider, or if they are to be included in the rent. Also, you both might need to kit out your parts of the building. In that case, we need to decide who's responsible for financing the designing and improvements you need to be able to carry out your businesses. Another factor we need to consider is payment for common areas like, er, parking and elevators. And, of course, we need to think about insurance and arrangements for ending the lease early – if, for example, your or your son's business outgrows the leased premises. Oh, um, there's something else, too, that could be important – we need to look at whether you might want to consider subletting if things don't work out. And, um – oh yes! – if and where you can put up a sign. And we mustn't forget clarifying who is responsible for paying property taxes. Oh, and, um, one more thing – just suppose your business doesn't do too well, and you want to sublet your part to your son or vice versa … we need to consider wording the lease so that …

MG: This is really pretty complex, isn't it? I think I've jotted down most of that, but could you just go over the last bit? How do you mean 'sublet to my son'? Isn't he going to be the landlord's tenant and not mine?

MH: Yes, but supposing you want to wind up your business and sublet your space to him. In that case, we need to make sure the wording of the lease won't prevent a computer-supply business becoming … er, what did you say?

MG: An animal-accessory shop.

MH: OK. That's about it for the moment. I'll send you a letter confirming our conversation and also a draft letter that I propose to send to the agent to get the ball rolling. If you want to add anything, or you think of anything else or have any queries in the meantime, you can give me a shout before I send the letter out.

MG: That's great. I'll wait to hear from you, then.

MH: I'll be in touch very soon. Goodbye for now.

Audio 6.2 22

Brigitte Trant: Good morning. I'm Brigitte Trant, and this is the helpline for the Moving Abroad website. How can I help you?

Thomas Maine: Well, I'm planning to move abroad with my family and open a small business – a restaurant, actually – and I know how important it is to get good legal representation. I'm just not that sure how to go about finding a good, reputable lawyer who deals with this sort of situation. Obviously I need someone I can trust to look after our interests in the best way. I was looking at your website and saw that you have a helpline, so I thought I'd give you a call.

BT: A good decision – I'm sure I can help you.

TM: Another point is – I don't really know the procedure. Do I need a lawyer based here in the UK, or a lawyer based in the country I'm moving to … or both?

BT: Right. Well, to start with, yours are very common questions. It can be a legal minefield out there when you're setting up a business in another country. There are so many different things to consider. And just to clarify your situation, I presume you want to buy the property you wish to use for your business as opposed to renting?

TM: Oh yes, and we want to live there, too.

BT: Then you'll be looking at a lot of important legal transactions and you'll need the right legal guidance. Firstly, regarding which or how many lawyers you'll need, that really depends on the country you're going to. What is vital is that the lawyer or lawyers you choose have a good understanding and experience of dealing with the commercial property laws and taxation systems in both countries. You may find that one lawyer will be all you need – or that the firm you choose has several specialist lawyers that can cover everything without you having to hire someone else in the actual country.

TM: I understand. So, are there any societies or organizations that I can contact for recommendations?

BT: Yes – there's the Law Society in the UK. They have lists of English lawyers working abroad and also they can tell you about lawyers in your local area who have the right experience. There's also the Federation of Overseas Property Developers, Agents and Consultants, and of course you could always get in touch with the British Consulate for your country – they have lists of English-speaking lawyers.

TM: Ah-ha. Can I be sure that the lawyers on these lists are reliable?

BT: There's no guarantee. These are simply lists, I'm afraid – you'll have to do some background checks yourself.

TM: So, what should I be checking for?

BT: Firstly, you must make sure that they've got the right knowledge, experience and qualifications. And – very important – that they're qualified to act in that country. Secondly, check the language skills. You want someone with both good English and good skills in the language of the country you're moving to. If that's not possible, make sure they use a good translation service.

TM: Ah, yes, I can see that's pretty important!

BT: When you've found someone, go to meet them and ask yourself if you like their manner, their way of dealing with people … and if you feel uncomfortable with this person for any reason, don't be afraid to say 'no' and look elsewhere.

TM: Can you give me an idea of how much I'm likely to pay for legal services?

BT: Mm, obviously fees vary from lawyer to lawyer and country to country, but you should be looking at between one and two per cent of the property price. And it's important to check this out first – don't just leave it and get a nasty surprise at the end of the deal! It can also give you an idea of how genuine the lawyer may be.

TM: This is all very useful – thanks.

BT: Oh, and one last thing. When you're looking for a good lawyer, recommendation is always a good way of doing it – recommendations from friends or colleagues who have used them, too. But a tip to remember: don't accept advice from anyone involved in the deal – the estate agent, developer or vendor. Never a good idea!

TM: Good advice! And thanks once again. You've been a great help!

Audio 7.1 23

Kate: Good afternoon, Charles. What can I do for you?

Charles: Well, I'm interested in setting up a company, but I'm not too sure what this involves, as I'm really new to all this. I've decided to go out on my own after all these years of working for another company.

K: OK, so what type of business do you have in mind? I presume that it's got something to do with what you've been working in – it's engineering, isn't it?

C: Yep, that's right, but I've been travelling a lot recently in Africa, and myself and my two brothers have decided to set up a company to supply water-drilling equipment and training for under-resourced countries. We have the knowledge and the expertise, so we've decided that this is what we want to do. It'll mean that we'll be tendering for jobs with various government departments and EU funders and donors, so we want to make sure that we have all the paperwork done professionally.

Audio 7.2 24

K: In my opinion, you should be thinking about forming a private company. And if so, then I think you should give some thought to being a CIC – a community interest company. This could well be appropriate for your requirements. There is, however, a feature known as *asset lock*, which means that its assets and property must be applied for the objects of the company only. So it would depend on whether you are in this to make money or for a community interest – that's up to you to decide. There are also specific rules about inward investment, such as limited dividends and limited interests payable on loans. One other thing to remember is that a private unlimited company cannot be a CIC.

C: OK, thanks. I'll go and have a chat with Joe and Henry about this. It would be really useful if you could send us some more detailed information on our options. We can go through it and then we'll put our heads together and decide which company would be the best for what we want to do. Then we'll come back to you and maybe you can set the necessary paperwork in motion for us. Is there a lot involved?

K: No, not really. Once you've made a decision about the type of company, then it's a matter of drafting the Memorandum of Association, with the various objects of the company, and the Articles of Association, with the rules for the running and regulation of the internal affairs of the company – though there are special requirements relating to Memoranda of Association for community interest companies, so I'll have to look into this further. I'll send you the information you need … then if you come back to me as soon as you've made a decision, I'll get going on some outline drafting. We can have another meeting then.

C: OK, I'll get back to you before the end of the week.

Audio 7.3

Extract 1 25

Well, I'm afraid that what you have in mind would be contrary to the law relating to directors' duties in respect of joint stock companies and private limited liability companies. You see, a director can't hold a controlling interest in another company with the same or a similar scope of business. So that rules out what you hope to do and, as your lawyer, I'm duty bound to advise you of the Czech law. However, if your company is in the not-for-profit sector, then that's a way round it. Then you could be on both boards, and I wouldn't foresee any problems.

Extract 2 26

It totally depends on why you are resigning. You see, under French law, you may be ordered to pay damages to repair the loss incurred by the company. But in your case, I can't see any problem. After all, the law doesn't require you to continue when you can't keep up to speed with what's going on. It's perfectly understandable. You should definitely resign well before the treatment starts, because when you're discharged, you won't be in a fit state to continue. Two weeks' clear notice should keep you well within the law.

Extract 3 27

Yes, I see, but the situation here in Italy is that you can't stay on. I'm sure you will be greatly missed, but the law is the law. It's a shame, particularly since you helped start it all from scratch and have seen it through some tricky situations – it must be hard to leave it behind when it's going as well as it is. Unfortunately, it's been three financial years. If you don't stand down, you'll be in trouble under Italian law, and that will affect you for any future positions in a similar role. But I'm sure that your hard work and experience, especially in the advertising field, has been appreciated and, in my opinion, you may well be re-elected, so I wouldn't worry too much.

Extract 4 28

I know this must be very frustrating for you. In all honesty, it's a pity you didn't come to me when you were negotiating the service agreement. I'd have made sure you were well aware that it was dependant on your staying on. You see, when you are no longer a managing director, you'll have no involvement. In your case, with your livelihood depending on your being able to get this business, you may well have reconsidered your decision to resign. Unfortunately, it's now too late for that, and I'm afraid there's nothing I can do.

Extract 5 29

Well, if you want to set it up in Poland, it must have a management board. I know it's different to other countries, but that's the law here. And I've been over this several times, if you remember … To reiterate what I said, if there are twenty-six shareholders, it means that this requirement stands. Under twenty-six is a different matter. If you refer to my letter of the fifth of March, you'll find that I laid out all the requirements quite clearly.

Audio 8.1 30

Mark: Hi, Helen, what can I do for you?
Helen: Hi, Mark, I'm so glad I caught you. You know my company's been hit by this recession, just like everyone else.
M: Yes, I'd heard.
H: Well, I want to increase the capital of the company to get us through. I'm not sure what the best way to go about this is, but I have to do something, otherwise we're going to go under.

Audio 8.2 31

M: OK, Helen. Let me take you through the basics, and then you can come to a decision and get back to me. I know that there are others involved, so it's important that you run this by them first before you make a decision. Um, firstly, I'm not too sure that raising share capital is the best way for you to go. I'd think about borrowing first and consider the different types of securities that would have to be given. I know things are tight all over the financial world right now, but you have a good operation, so I don't foresee any major problems on that front. Um, another thing that you might consider is borrowing from directors and shareholders, either formally – perhaps granting them a debenture – or informally, with just book-keeping records, such as a directors' loan account. Lending money or assets to the company can be an alternative to putting it in as share capital.

Audio 8.3 32

H: I don't think that will work – things are a bit tight for everyone at the moment. Um, if we go with the formal option, what's involved?
M: OK, well, in that case, it will mean issuing debentures to secure the loan.
H: Can you put that in simple terms?
M: OK. Um, a debenture, put in simple terms, is the traditional name given to a loan agreement where the borrower is a company. A debenture will usually set out the terms of the loan: the amount borrowed, repayment terms, interest, charges securing the loan, provisions for protecting and insuring the property, etc., and terms for enforcement if the company defaults. Debentures are usually secured by charges on the company's property, but they don't have to be. Debentures, as such, don't have to be registered, but charges securing them do.
H: OK, I think I've got that. Essentially what you're saying is go and borrow the money, register the debenture, and then give a charge over the company's assets to the lending institution.

Audio 8.4 33

M: Yep, that's about it, but there are different types of charges that you would have to consider – such as fixed or floating charges – and they'll have different impacts, depending on which one you go for, or rather which one the lending institution goes for, as they are really in the driving seat on this one. A fixed charge is usually over the premises or the company's debtor book. In the former case, the charge is like a mortgage; in the latter, the company assigns the debtor book, and the institution buys the outstanding invoices and lends money against them. A floating charge is over the company's remaining assets, such as stock, fixtures and fittings, vehicles and any assets not subject to a fixed charge. Test the water first, but don't sign anything. Come back to me when you have a clearer picture of what the institution wants.
H: Will do – thanks a million. I owe you!

Audio 8.5

Extract 1 34

Jane: So, Carl is moving to the US. I'm not surprised. There's so much work there at the moment, isn't there, Mike?
Mike: Yes. You know, there are massive restructurings underway in the US and Canada, which means a huge workload for the lawyers. But as well as the work, the lawyers there have to deal with all the media attention, too. In effect, the lawyer has now become the spokesperson for the client company. This is so different to what we're used to! It's another added pressure.

Jane: As if there wasn't enough pressure as it is! Things are changing so quickly in the world of restructuring, aren't they? Before this recession, if a big company was in trouble and had to go for a restructuring of any kind, like filing for bankruptcy, it was a pretty cut-and-dried case. Now, there are so many other issues all popping up at the same time. Restructurings are crossing industries and borders, and for lawyers, we're trying to find solutions for problems that no one has ever seen before. You're right – it's added pressure for lawyers, as traditionally we aren't used to making decisions on the go. And we're dealing with crises on a minute-by-minute basis.

Extract 2 🟢 35

Katy: Morris, what do you think is important when a company is looking for legal help with restructuring?

Morris: Well, these days, it's trust and confidence that's important. Even for companies in a debtor position, using their usual outside counsel for a restructuring might not be the wisest choice. When a company runs out of time, that's often considered the fastest thing to do, but it's not necessarily the best. Facing financial distress is probably the most serious matter a company will encounter in its history, since the life of the company is at stake. Debtor companies probably – and thankfully – don't have a lot of experience in restructuring. The main concern is to get the right advisors in place, sooner rather than later.

K: And the right advisors would be … ?

M: Definitely restructuring specialists. It's a very specialized area, with the all the legislation for companies, creditors' arrangements, bankruptcy and insolvency. The lawyers have to know what they can and can't do, how the court process works and have a fair bit of experience to be able to provide high-level strategic and tactical advice to a company, creditor or bondholder.

Extract 3 🟢 36

Paula: How's work going at the moment, James?

James: Well, as you know, we specialize in restructuring, and for quite a long time, things weren't going so well. A lot of restructuring firms saw their businesses shrink, but it's a whole different story today! Our firm is working at full capacity, and things are getting very competitive.

P: Yes, I imagine companies undergoing restructuring tend to turn to law firms with good reputations in that field.

J: Exactly. And when dealing with finding credit, law firms that have long-standing relationships with lenders, financial advisors or accounting firms serving as monitors are typically retained in restructurings. So, yes – we're doing pretty well at the moment, thank you!

Audio 9.1 🟢 37

Martin James: Hi, Denise. I've got a bit of a problem and at this stage I need some very general advice on what I should do to avoid any possible fines or penalties.

Denise Howard: OK.

MJ: Well, it involves teddy bears.

DH: Teddy bears?!

MJ: Yes. You see, I'm importing the 'Love You Always' teddy bear. It has a heart that lights up when you hug it.

DH: Sounds lovely!

MJ: It is. It runs on rechargeable batteries, which we sell with a charger along with the bears. We've been doing a lot of advertising for the Christmas market, and it's been a huge seller – a big hit with kids and adults alike. At least, it was.

DH: What do you mean, 'was'?

MJ: Well, there was a manufacturing fault. The manufacturers didn't use the correct glue, and quite a few of the bears' eyes came off. We've had to do a product recall of 10,000 bears in Ireland! Well, that's bad enough, but what's even worse is disposing of the things. It's a real nightmare. I mean, we can hardly take 10,000 bears to a landfill, can we? And there's the added complication of some EU Directive on batteries. Each bear has two rechargeable batteries and one charger, so that's 20,000 batteries and 10,000 chargers to be got rid of. At the moment, my house and office are stuffed with the things.

DH: Right. There are two Directives covering this situation. Well, three if you count the Battery Directive, which is on the way but not in force yet. So, at the moment, we have the WEEE Directive 96 of 2002. This is the Waste Electrical and Electronic Equipment Directive. Then there's the Restriction on the use of certain Hazardous Substances in Electrical and Electronic Equipment, the RoHS Directive 95 of 2002. And you're right – if the bears are covered by one or both of these Directives, you may well have to make special arrangements for correct disposal or else you could possibly be in line for a penalty – or, at the very least, bad publicity.

MJ: How do I know if these Directives are applicable?

DH: Well, it's not that clear cut. The Directives apply to equipment that's dependent on electric current in order to work properly, like an electric kettle or an electric iron. I presume you don't or can't plug the bear in if the light in his heart is getting weak?

MJ: No, it's not a plug-in bear, it only works on rechargeable batteries.

DH: Right. If your bear was a plug-in bear and you could turn the power on and off, then it would obviously be covered. But this is a really grey area because of the rechargeable batteries. They have to be charged with electricity and they won't work without it, and the bear won't work without the batteries. Off the top of my head, I think you're still covered by the Directives because the bear doesn't work without batteries, and these are rechargeable. So before you do anything, I think we need to discuss this in more depth. I'll put you through to my secretary and you can make an appointment to come in next week.

Audio 9.2 🟢 38

Mrs Clarke: Good morning, Mr Davies. What can I do for you?

Mr Davies: Thank you for meeting with me, Mrs Clarke. I'm really concerned about a situation that has arisen. I represent an organization called Green Concern, and we're seriously worried about a site known locally as the Cassani site. There is serious water and soil contamination – the pollution is coming from potentially toxic waste from industrial and disposal facilities nearby.

MC: OK. And who is this affecting?

MD: It's directly affecting the residents of the area adjoining the site, who depend on the water and soil for farming. They believe that they haven't been sufficiently involved in the decision-making processes in respect of the disposal of the waste, and they also maintain that the authorities haven't given them access to sufficient information.

MC: And your organization is representing the farmers?

MD: Mm-hm. That's right. We believe that the 'polluter pays' principle laid down in EU Directive 35 of 2004 has been infringed. There's also the matter of provision for public participation under EU Directive 4 of 2003, as well as access to justice in environmental matters under EU Directive 35 of 2003.

MC: You certainly know your directives!

MD: Well, we've got certain experience in this field, but we really need some legal advice from an environmental lawyer like yourself. Could you advise us on what course of action we should take?

MC: Mm, right. Well, there are a number of issues here to start off with. Um, firstly, the 'polluter pays' principle is what it says – it's a principle or a framework for principles guiding the Community Environmental policy. It doesn't have a legal basis that can be invoked for action. And it can't be used as a basis for determining or deciding non-compliance.

MD: Surely there's something we can do?

Audio transcripts 103

MC: Well, the principle does form the basis of the Environmental Liability Directive. The main objective of this is to prevent imminent damage and to restore damage already caused. Um, I'd need dates and some more information in relation to the contamination. I'd also need to know the degrees of contamination, the various contaminants, um, and their effect on the water and soil quality. The dates and times are important because the Environmental Liability Directive doesn't apply to damage caused by an event happening before the thirtieth of April 2007 or damage caused after the thirtieth of April 2007 that is a result of an event that took place before that date.

MD: Well, on that, I can tell you that this has been going on for a long time. I'm not too sure, but going on memory, I think it started in or around 2001 or 2002, and the authorities then tendered for a company to come in and clean up the mess.

MC: OK. Those dates are critical, and I'd need more information before being able to advise. Can I ask you why nothing was done about legal proceedings until now?

MD: We only became aware of this when some farmers came to us because their animals were getting sick and they asked us to take a look at the situation. Basically, the farmers couldn't afford to take the matter to court before. If they'd failed, they'd have had to pay costs.

MC: What you need to do is to have a meeting with the farmers involved and get information about dates, times, degrees of contamination and action taken by them over the period of time involved. Then I'd be able to give preliminary advice on a course of action, but it really is a bit premature of me to advise without these details.

Answer key

1 Intellectual property

Reading (page 10)
1 1 • To give statutory expression to the moral and economic rights of creators in their creations and to give statutory expression to the rights of the public in accessing those creations
   • To promote creativity and the dissemination and application of the results of such creativity and to encourage fair trade
   2 The two legal categories mentioned are industrial property and copyright.
   3 They give rise to varying degrees of protection and enforcement.
2 A right is created by statute or by international treaty.
  A duty is imposed to comply with terms of the statute or an international treaty.
  An obligation arises by virtue of the requirement to adhere to the statute or treaty terms and to enforce it.
3 1 promote   2 distinct   3 results in   4 statutory   5 enacted
   6 namely
4 *Suggested answers*
  industrial property: commercial names, designations, disclosure, layout designs, patents, register, trademarks
  copyright: infringement, licence, performance, reproduction, translation
6 1 Authors' rights relate to the creator of the work. Copyright refers to the act of making copies of the work.
   2 No, the invention does not have to be physically in existence.
   3 Protection for an invention gives a monopoly right to *exploit an idea*, so the duration is about 20 years, because it is only the exploitation of the idea that is protected. Copyright protection, on the other hand, prevents unauthorised use of the *expression* of the ideas, so the duration of protection can be much longer.
   4 Through registration of the invention
   5 Because a created work is considered protected as soon as it exists.
7 1 terms   2 exploit   3 licence   4 distinct   5 aware   6 gives rise
8 1 com<u>pete</u>   2 per<u>mit</u>   3 <u>remedy</u>   4 m<u>o</u>nopolize   5 solve
   6 dis<u>close</u>

Listening (page 12)
4 1 true   2 true   3 false
5 1 Socially, through the tennis club (but she doesn't know him very well, as they are not on first-name terms).
   2 She doesn't want to make her complaint too formal, as she's unsure about what can be done.
   3 They have been put together for the students on a course to use. They contain articles, notes or syllabi, sample test questions and excerpts.
   4 For the material to be reproduced only in course packs
   5 She's angry with the copy shop for making more copies than necessary and selling them on for profit.
   6 He suggests Professor Daykin write out the details so that he can look at the matter further.
6 **a** 1 c   2 h   3 g   4 f   5 b   6 e   7 a   8 d
  b 1 D   2 H   3 H   4 D   5 D   6 H   7 H   8 H

Speaking 1 (page 13)
2 **a** 1 SC   2 E   3 A   4 E   5 A   6 SC   7 A   8 E   9 A   10 SC

Writing (page 14)
2 **c** 1 further   2 as well as   3 Following this   4 Recently
   5 Furthermore   6 already   7 concerned   8 hear
   9 sincerely
3 c, e, f, d, b, g, a
4 *Suggested answers*
  (Some expressions may be useful for more than one point.)
  a We will be left with no alternative but to …
    Alternatively, …
    It is our intention to …
    We require you to …
  b It may well be that …
  c In relation to …
    We are instructed that …
    Our client informs us that …
    On behalf of …
  d You will be liable for …
  e One of the terms provides that …
  f Our client has suffered …
    This is covered by …
    The terms and conditions specifically provide …
  g Your response was …

Exam practice
Reading
1 D   2 D   3 C   4 B   5 B   6 A   7 B   8 C   9 B   10 D   11 A   12 C
Listening
1 copied   2 faster; better   3 inevitable   4 French   5 handbag; shoe   6 admit liability   7 inexpensive   8 bags; belts   9 public

2 Competition law

Reading 1 (page 18)
1 1 • Agreements or practices that restrict free trading
     • Anticompetitive practices that lead to one firm dominating a market
   2 Antitrust law
   3 No. Any business, regardless of size, needs to know about competition law.
   4 a Risk of fine (10% group global turnover) or being sued by customers
     b Director disqualification orders or criminal scanctions
   5 US antitrust law and EU competition law
2 1 free trading / competition   2 a market   3 trusts
   4 its obligations   5 findings   6 the risk / the possibility
   7 the risk   8 its rights   9 its position
3 **a** 1 c   2 e   3 g   4 h   5 a   6 i   7 b   8 d   9 f
4 1 so   2 so   3 such   4 Such   5 so

Reading 2 (page 20)
1 1 A *presumption* starts from a specific legal basis; if something is *deemed* to be X, it is found to be X based on certain criteria.
   2 • a document ensuring a process is carried out (a promise)
     • a business in the market
   3 A business with most control of the market in a specific sector
2 1 Belgium, Cyprus, France
   2 a Austria   b Austria   c Bulgaria   d Czech Republic
     e France   f Belgium   g Austria
     The figures all relate to percentages which show an undertaking is dominant or has market share.
3 1 Czech Republic   2 Austria   3 Czech Republic   4 Austria

Listening (page 22)

1. 1 A method used by lawyers to help focus on facts, issues and the law
   2 Elements, facts, factual propositions
   3 Elements are necessary factors for particular aspects of law to be considered; factual propositions are facts that make up elements.
2. 1 E 2 FP 3 F 4 E 5 F 6 F 7 FP 8 F 9 F
3. a 1 Jupiter Electronics
   2 Selling electrical goods
   3 Baker Retail, Appliance Zone, Cool Places
   4 A chain of department stores, a national manufacturer, a distributor
   5 They conspired either not to sell to the client or to do so only at discriminatory prices and unfavourable terms.
   6 That it was a justified action – Jupiter Electronics could charge more, as its branches are open 24 hours.
   b 1 illegal 2 conspiracy 3 forbids 4 commerce 5 monopoly
   c TVs **20%** and **refrigerators** 40% over the cost to others. Very **small** business, established for many years, but size of business **not** relevant.
4. 1 early January 2 25th May 3 five; 29th June
   4 12th, 17th and 28th December 5 ten 6 380s
5. 1 exactly 2 say 3 that 4 something 5 Did 6 just
6. 1 What was that name again?
   2 And when did she phone?
   3 And your point is … ?

Writing (page 24)

2. 1 c 2 b 3 e 4 g 5 f 6 a 7 d
3. 1 b 2 g 3 a 4 f

Speaking (page 25)

3.

–ive	–able	–ant	–ial
abusive competitive restrictive	enforceable favourable variable	dominant	commercial financial influential

–al	–ory	–ic
criminal economical	discriminatory predatory statutory	economic

Exam practice

Reading
1 didn't 2 able 3 order 4 such/these 5 well 6 Despite
7 much 8 for/against 9 makes 10 their 11 it 12 not

Listening
1 A 2 C 3 C 4 C 5 B 6 C

3 Employment law

Reading 1 (page 28)

1. 1 International employment law is changing to fit the needs of increasingly global business.
   2 When the labour legislation or practice of a country has reached a certain level, it may be desirable for that country to ratify a convention. The reason for this is that there may be an international standard which corresponds to the existing national situation.
   3 Many conventions are based on the notion of social justice.
2. 1 perspective 2 transactions 3 facility 4 workforce
   5 drafting 6 terminating 7 benefits 8 unions 9 reductions
   10 severance 11 pension 12 race 13 dismissal
3. 1 discrimination 2 pensions 3 recruitment 4 disability
   5 discrimination 6 redundancy 7 dismissal
   8 employment contracts
4. a 1 consolidate 2 ratify 3 terminate 4 discriminate
   5 legislate 6 regulate
   b ratify
   c The stress patterns are different between the nouns and the verbs. In the nouns, the stress falls on the penultimate syllable. In the verbs, the stress falls on the third-from-last syllable.

Reading 2 (page 30)

1. 1 An act is part of domestic legislation and has a validity and obligations in a national context. A convention is an agreement ratified internationally.
   2 An article is in a convention, a section is in an act.
3. A 2 (Art. 2, Part 1, Convention No. 87)
   B 7 (Art. 1, Part 1, Convention No. 98)
   C 6 (Art. 2, Part 4, Convention No. 138)
4. 1 thereof 2 consent 3 in respect of 4 by reason of
   5 provisions 6 refrain from 7 notwithstanding 8 enjoy
   9 such 10 relinquish 11 otherwise 12 authorize
5. 1 undertakes 2 suppress 3 view 4 recourse 5 measure
   6 hereinafter

Listening (page 32)

2. 1 true 2 false 3 false 4 true 5 false 6 true 7 true
   8 false 9 true
3. 1 M 2 M 3 P 4 M 5 P 6 M 7 M 8 M 9 M 10 M
4. 1 b 2 e 3 a 4 f 5 g 6 h 7 d 8 c

Speaking 1 (page 33)

2. a 1 Hear 2 Allow 3 build 4 agreement 5 effect
   6 Explain 7 Ask for 8 positions 9 Identify 10 Probe
   11 trade-offs 12 Name
   b *Suggested answers*
   introduction: 1, 2, 3
   first joint session: 6, 7, 8, 9, 10, 12
   private sessions: 5, 8, 9, 10, 11
   final joint session: 4

Writing (page 34)

1. *Suggested answer*
   f, e, d, a, b, c, g
2. 1 O/RC 2 A 3 O 4 RC 5 O 6 RF 7 S 8 RC/O 9 RC
   10 RF 11 O 12 A

Exam practice

Reading
1 F 2 B 3 E 4 H 5 G 6 A 7 D

Listening
1 c 2 b 3 c 4 a 5 b

4 Contract law 1

Reading 1 (page 38)

1. a 1 To make it as complete and precise as possible
   2 They can be expensive and time consuming and can damage reputations.
   3 See bullet list in the document on page 39.
2. 1 To allow the contract terms to be clear
   2 A rule of contractual interpretation where the party that insisted on an ambiguous term being in a contract won't get the benefit of it
   3 Keep it exactly the same.
   4 They are familiar to those involved and can save time.
   5 Dates and currencies
   6 CISG, UNIDROIT principles and ICC incoterms
3. 1 am<u>bi</u>guous 2 a<u>vai</u>lable 3 confi<u>den</u>tial 4 <u>lia</u>ble
   5 ad<u>vi</u>sable 6 <u>ty</u>pical

4 1 warranty: specific written guarantee to cover repairs/
      replacement, etc.
      guarantee: more general
   2 set: group of things that belong together
      group: more general
   3 terms: what a contract does or doesn't do
      clause: where the terms are contained in a contract
   4 duty: something that has to be done
      right: something that is allowed
   5 termination: the ending of something
      finalization: the completion of something
   6 comprise: these things form …
      include: these things are part of …
   7 remedies: methods of getting redress and compensation
      arbitration: form of dispute resolution, alternative to court
   8 construed: interpreted
      believed: thought to be
   9 numerous: a lot of
      a number of: several
5 1 warranty 2 remedies 3 duty 4 Termination
   5 A number of

Reading 2 (page 40)

3 1 essential 2 voluntary 3 consensual 4 distinguishes
   5 bind 6 common 7 determine 8 enforceable 9 ratified
   10 uniformed 11 irrespective of

Listening (page 41)

1 1 Agreements, rights, obligations and remedies
   2 Termination, interpretation, possible litigation
2 1 a   2 b, e   3 d
3 1 pairs 2 about 3 fundamental 4 complete 5 perform
   6 render 7 commence 8 terminate 9 active 10 short
   11 verbs 12 compound
4 *Suggested answers*
   1 The misrepresentation made the contract unenforceable.
   2 The chairman began the proceedings by reading the agenda.
   3 The client discontinued his relationship with his lawyers
     immediately.
   4 The firm of lawyers was established in 1960. It has many
     highly qualified partners and extensive premises, with meeting
     rooms and other facilities for clients.
   5 The tenant must pay the rent promptly.
5 *Suggested answers*
   1 try 2 find out 3 send 4 keep 5 consider 6 tell 7 get
   8 tell 9 use
7 1 b   2 a   3 c
8 1 f   2 a   3 d   4 g   5 c   6 b   7 e

Speaking (page 44)

2 b 1 c 2 d 3 h 4 g 5 e 6 f 7 i 8 l 9 j 10 a 11 b
      12 k
3 1 critical 2 end up 3 anticipate 4 live up to 5 research
   6 drive towards 7 being attentive 8 hold off 9 raise an issue
   10 tough

Exam practice
Reading
1 by 2 whatever 3 sure 4 it 5 which 6 any
7 caused/incurred 8 what 9 up 10 or 11 would/will
12 rather
Listening
1 E 2 F 3 C 4 A 5 D
6 B 7 A 8 E 9 C 10 D

5 Contract law 2

Reading 1 (page 48)

2 1 Failure to supply goods, failure to perform a service
   2 Fundamental breach: serious breach of a fundamental term or
     total failure to perform
     Anticipatory breach: contract repudiated before performance
     is due. Repudiation can be express or implied.
   3 Bringing an action for damages for breach
     Completing contract then suing for damages
3 1 implied repudiation 2 repudiated 3 anticipatory breach
   4 fundamental breach 5 frustration
5 1 serve to 2 terminate 3 elect 4 innocent 5 perform
   6 give rise to 7 treat 8 fundamental 9 valid
   10 subsequently 11 convey 12 hires
6 1 performance 2 supply 3 discharge 4 termination
   5 repudiation 6 treatment 7 failure 8 implication
   Supply and *discharge* remain the same.
7 1 implication 2 failure 3 treatment 4 supply
   5 termination

Reading 2 (page 50)

2 b 1 Courts are far more inclined to uphold this method of
        agreement.
      2 B2C contracts are between a business and a consumer;
        B2B contracts are between two businesses.
      3 Data protection and privacy issues
      4 UNCITRAL Model Law on Electronic Commerce
      5 Because it reduces costs for new businesses to access new
        markets.
      6 Awareness of terms and their clarity, size and location on
        the website
      7 Law governing electronic signatures; international treaty on
        Jurisdiction and Enforcements of Judgements; global
        agreement on e-commerce tax regulations

Reading 3 (page 51)

2 a 2   b 2   c 1   d 3   e 3   f 2   g 1
3 1 b   2 d   3 f   4 c   5 e   6 a

Listening (page 52)

1 b 1 liquidated damages 2 stipulated damages
      3 special damages 4 reliance damages
      5 consequential damages 6 specific performance
2 1 P 2 P 3 S 4 P 5 S 6 P 7 S 8 P 9 S 10 S 11 P 12 P

Writing (page 52)

1 b 1 Loss 2 Defective 3 handy 4 waterproof 5 rubber
      6 selling point 7 conformity

Exam practice
Reading
1 contractual 2 consideration 3 heading 4 basis 5 restrictions
6 solely 7 improvements 8 expenditure 9 expectation
10 profitable
Listening
1 unnecessary risk 2 time 3 in-house 4 IT 5 punctuation
6 disputes 7 guarantee 8 tips 9 first

6 Real property law

Reading 1 (page 56)

2 1 estate   2 leasehold   3 freehold   4 heir   5 tenant   6 rent
7 easement   8 licence   9 landlord

3 a 1 An estate limited to a man and his heirs; the most absolute interest in land that someone can own. It has the potential to last forever and will end only when the owner (or the heirs of his body as opposed to non-blood relatives) dies intestate.
2 An estate limited to a man and the heirs of his body; it can only be given to one person and his direct heirs.
3 An estate to one person for his own life
4 An estate to be held for the duration of another's life
5 A reversion happens where a landowner (A) grants away some estate lesser than his own which is to be enjoyed in possession by someone else (B). If A grants to B for life, then when B dies, the estate reverts back to A.
6 A remainder happens when the grantor creates an estate to be enjoyed in possession in the future by someone else other than himself. For example, if A (who owns the fee simple of Blackacre) conveys Blackacre to B for life, remainder to C, B has a life estate and C has the remainder, which he will be able to enjoy when B dies.

Reading 2 (page 56)

2 1 d   2 c   3 a   4 e   5 b
3 1 c   2 d   3 b/f   4 e   5 g   6 h   7 a   8 f/b

Listening (page 58)

2 1 preliminary advice   2 agent's details   3 security deposit
4 directly   5 in the rent   6 the lease early   7 subletting
8 wording   9 draft   10 confirming
3 1 going out on my own   2 go hand in hand
3 come back to me   4 work out   5 part of   6 shared
7 kit out   8 carry out   9 don't work out   10 jotted
11 go over   12 wind up your business   13 get the ball rolling
14 give me a shout

Reading 3 (page 60)

2 1 F (He has not yet purchased it.)   2 F (There is no real need for it in Germany.)   3 F (Buyers, lenders and lawyers also benefit from it.)   4 T   5 F (It makes it easier to get financial backing.)
3 1 perspective   2 place   3 recall   4 return   5 moment   6 fair

Exam practice

Reading
1 C   2 A   3 D   4 C   5 D   6 B
Listening
1 B   2 A   3 C   4 C   5 C

7 Company law 1

Lead-in (page 64)

The four main types of company are: private company limited by shares, private company limited by guarantee, private unlimited company, public limited company. See Exercises 2–7 for features.

Listening 1 (page 64)

1 1 No
2 Engineering
3 In Africa
4 The company will supply water-drilling equipment and training for under-resourced countries and will tender for contracts to do this work.
5 Its main competition will be from other companies that tender for jobs with government departments and EU funders and donors.

Reading 1 (page 65)

1 1 e   2 b   3 h   4 d   5 g   6 f   7 a   8 c
2 1 extensive   2 duration   3 dissolution   4 minimal   5 deemed
6 terminate   7 retain   8 time-consuming   9 dissolved

Reading 2 (page 66)

1 a A 2   B 3   C 1
   b A (a recommendation) should   B (a statute) must
      C (an agreement) shall
2 1 sustainability   2 linked   3 non-financial   4 certain   5 to
6 manifestly   7 also   8 contribute   9 while   10 adjustment
11 such   12 specified   13 devote   14 consent   15 on
16 commercial   17 other   18 its
3 Suggested answers
1 salaries/payment   2 make sure/provide   3 important
4 postponed/put off   5 in addition   6 get back/claim back
7 obviously   8 agrees/contracts   9 stops   10 in excess of
11 their whole time/their complete time   12 sign/be a part of
13 buy

Reading 3 (page 67)

3 1 false   2 true   3 false   4 false   5 true   6 false   7 false   8 true

Listening 2 (page 68)

1 b 1 community interest company: specific rules about inward investment, such as limited dividends and limited interests payable on loans; a private unlimited company cannot be a CIC; special requirements relating to Memoranda and Association for community interest companies
2 asset lock: the company's assets and property must be applied for the objects of the company only
3 Memorandum of Association: states the objects of the company
4 Articles of Association: state the rules for the running and regulation of the internal affairs of the company
2 1 K (forming a private company)
2 K (being a CIC)
3 K (client's/Charles's requirements)
4 K (whether the clients (Charles and his brothers) want to make money or to operate a business for the good of the community)
5 C (details about options available to Charles and his brothers)
6 C (the information the lawyer is going to send)
7 C (the brothers making a decision)
8 C (drafting the required documents after a decision has been made)
9 K (requirements of Memoranda of Association for CICs)
10 K (when the clients have made a decision)
11 K (making a start on the necessary drafting of the company documents)

Exam practice

Reading
1 C   2 B   3 A   4 C   5 C   6 A   7 C   8 D   9 B   10 C   11 B
12 C
Listening
1 E   2 A   3 C   4 F   5 B   6 E   7 F   8 A   9 D   10 B

8 Company law 2

Reading 1 (page 72)

2 1 a response   2 expand   3 timing   4 as   5 overall
6 maintain   7 remedy   8 falling   9 speed up   10 reject
11 take   12 scope   13 spin-off   14 back   15 entire
16 operates
3 1 It depends on the reasons why a company might want to restructure, such as a response to market circumstances, either to take opportunities for expansion or to contract operations to preserve profitably in recessionary times.

2 Creditors, shareholders, employees and other stakeholders
3 Declining or stagnating sales, accounting losses or a falling stock price
4 By being in a position to reject unfavourable leases and to sell unwanted assets in a competitive auction
5 By merging, consolidating or acquiring other companies or other activities which result in enlargement
6 When high growth is being held back by a parent company.

4 1 prevailing   2 overall   3 recessionary
   4 Declining / Stagnating   5 default   6 unwanted

5 *Suggested answers*
1 There were significant accounting losses, so the company was wound up / put into liquidation.
2 The company was looking for new business opportunities and decided to expand / merge with an existing company / take over another company which would be beneficial to its operation.
3 An equity spin-off was considered because the company wanted to increase its profitability by expanding each of its smaller companies / concentrate on developing some aspects of the business operated through smaller companies.

Reading 2 (page 74)

2 1 A lawyer may be required to either defend the debtor or act for a creditor in relation to: the accuracy of the amount claimed; the entry of judgement against the debtor by the creditor; the registration of the judgement against the debtor's property and proceedings for the sale of the property of the debtor to realize the amount of the judgement for the creditor.
2 Usually if there is no written agreement and two or more persons are carrying on business with goal of making a profit, a partnership may be deemed to be in existence.
3 In a partnership, all partners are jointly and severally liable for all debts of the partnership to the full extent of their assets.
4 In a limited company, the shareholders are only liable for company debts to the extent of any unpaid sums due on their shares. Unless directors have given personal guarantees, they are not liable for the company's debts so long as they run the company lawfully.

3 1 to wind up: to liquidate a business that is losing money
to write off: to realize that a debt is uncollectible and to abandon any attempts to collect it
2 in the case of: referring to a specific situation / set of facts / person
in respect of: referring to a specific thing
3 to dissolve: to officially end a business agreement / arrangement
to go bankrupt: to reach the stage of being insolvent and unable to pay debts
4 jointly retained: where two professionals are hired by one client to work together for that client
a joint venture: where two or more companies / business entities enter into a temporary partnership for a particular business enterprise
5 personal guarantee: a legally enforceable promise given by an individual to pay any debts outstanding on a loan from a financial institution
liability: a legal responsibility for paying for something / some event caused where there is financial loss
6 debt: money outstanding and due for payment
judgement: a court ruling after hearing evidence
7 assets: anything of value owned by a business
profits: money made by a business after deduction of all expenses
8 in relation to: referring to a specific set of facts, situation, person or thing
to the extent of: to the amount of

9 regarded as: to think about someone / something in a particular way, e.g. *He was regarded (by people) as being very intelligent.*
construed as: to draw a conclusion / interpret from circumstances / behaviour / writing, e.g. *His exclamation was construed as frustration. / The document was construed in her favour.*

4 1 from; to   2 for   3 against   4 as   5 off
5 a 1 d   2 c   3 e   4 b   5 a

Reading 3 (page 76)
2 1 D   2 A   3 C   4 B   5 E

Listening (page 77)

2 a Helen is contacting Mark because she wants to increase the capital of the company. She is concerned that if she doesn't, the company will go under.
  b 1 Helen can't make this decision herself (she needs Mark's advice, and there are others who need to be consulted).
    2 Mark doesn't think that raising share capital is the best option (he thinks she should look at borrowing money).
    3 correct
    4 correct
    5 correct
  c 1 terms   2 amount   3 terms   4 securing   5 provisions
    6 enforcement   7 defaults
  d Mark's final advice is to find out what charge (fixed or floating) the lending institution wants, but not to sign anything until she gets further legal advice.

3 a 1 gone under   2 run it by   3 set(s) out   4 get back
     5 go about   6 took us through   7 get through   8 go for

Reading 4 (page 79)
1 1 B   2 B   3 C
2 1 Just a very quick line to …   2 things have gone really sour
  3 We're going to have a fight on our hands to …
  4 as far as I'm concerned   5 go ahead
  6 I would really appreciate …
3 1 A, B   2 A, B, C   3 B   4 C
4 1 rebut   2 recognize   3 conduct   4 achieve
   5 initiate / oppose   6 pursue

Speaking 1 (page 81)
2 b 1 b 2 e 3 g 4 a 5 d 6 c 7 i 8 h 9 f 10 k 11 j
     12 l
4 1 As   2 While   3 because   4 just   5 More importantly
   6 While   7 also   8 Finally   9 but   10 in order

Exam Practice
Reading
1 personally   2 unlawful   3 contravention   4 obligations
5 proceedings   6 arises / arose   7 voluntary   8 objective
9 survival   10 detrimental   11 Furthermore   12 imprisonment

Listening
1 A   2 B   3 B   4 C   5 C   6 B

9 Environmental law

Reading 1 (page 86)
1 1 b   2 c   3 a   4 d
2 *Suggested answers*
(Technically, all modules would touch on topics 1–6, but some would deal with them in more detail than others. Learners should be encouraged to justify their selection as to why.)
1 A1 (sources of international environmental law, governance), A2 (environmental damage and state responsibility, civil liability for damage, environmental disputes, human rights), A3 (marine environment protection, conservation, principles and enforcement), A4 (environment and trade); B1, B2, B3, B4 (all if within the jurisdiction of the EU).

2 **A1** (sources of international law, governance institutions and jurisdiction issues), **A2** (environment and human rights), **A3** (marine protection, conservation and principles of enforcement, hazardous waste management and enforcement), **A4** (environment and trade, cross-border pollution management and penalty enforcement), **B1** (if within the jurisdiction of the EU: shared responsibility, environmental policy, 'polluter pays' principle, integrating environmental issues with economic policy, aspects of the 'precautionary principle'), **B2** (legal basis for environmental laws), **B3** (if within the jurisdiction of the EU), **B4** (rights to environmental information, participation and justice, human rights, environmental rights embedded in national constitutions)

3 **A1** (development and sources of international environmental law, governance institutions and jurisdiction (relevant for compliance)), **A2**, **A3**, **A4** (cross-border pollution management and penalty enforcement), **B1** (shared responsibility, principles of environmental policy (if the regulations are affected by EU considerations), integrating environmental issues with economic policy (as agriculture may form part of economic policy), **B2** (if within the jurisdiction of the EU), **B3** (challenging the validity of EU legislation, enforcement by the Commission, state responsibility for breaches, penalties), **B4** (rights to information, participation, human rights, environmental rights embedded in national constitutions).

4 **A1** (environmental governance and jurisdiction issues, sustainable development), **A2** (environmental damage, resolution of disputes, environment and human rights), **A3** (conservation and biological diversity, principles and enforcement), **A4** (cross-border pollution management (if relevant)), **B1** (market-based instruments (if re-zoning is for economic reasons), integrating environmental issues with economic policy), **B2**, **B3**, **B4**.

5 **A1**, **A2**, **A3**, **A4** (if dealing internationally), **B1**, **B2**, **B3**, **B4** (if within EU and extension of EU law internationally).

6 All modules are relevant, depending on what is being considered.

Reading 2 (page 87)
1 A Course A   B Course B   C Course A   D Course B
  E Course A
2 1 D   2 D   3 B   4 A   5 D, E   6 E   7 A
3 1 suit   2 token   3 balance   4 score   5 overriding   6 big
  7 point   8 hand   9 tough   10 lean   11 factor   12 pushed

Reading 3 (page 90)
1 1 adequacy   2 exclusion   3 partial   4 preliminary
  5 presumption   6 dissemination   7 refusal   8 central
  9 periodic
2 1 The Commission refers to Articles 1–7 because they are relevant for the proceedings. They cover the agencies responsible for, and the processes for access to, information; the making available of information; the cost requirements of same; the categories of persons entitled to information; the process for appeal against refusal to deliver information.
  2 The Commission is challenging the adequacy of German legislation in bringing the requirements of the Directive into national law.
  3 The challenge is based on the following grounds:
  • the exclusion of judicial bodies from enforcing the Directive
  • the way information should be made available under the terms of the Directive
  • the review processes that can be used when information is not made available.
3 1 assumption   2 optional   3 financial   4 conspiracy
  5 realization   6 imaginary/imaginative   7 denial   8 collusion
  9 historic(al)

4 1 transposition   2 scope   3 provisions   4 preamble
  5 interest   6 stipulates   7 levied   8 material
5 1 material   2 preamble   3 levy   4 interest   5 scope

Reading 4 (page 92)
1 1 interpretation   2 criteria   3 origin   4 applied   5 protection
  6 Vulnerable   7 drain   8 concentration   9 eliminating
  10 affected
2 *Suggested answers*
  1 The High Court has referred the case for an interpretation and validity of a directive.
  2 The issue that community law cannot provide precise criteria for establishing whether agricultural pollution makes a significant contribution to the pollution and therefore the Directive may be applied in different ways by Member States
  3 The Article in question concerns protection of waters against pollution by nitrates.
  4 The firm's argument is that nitrates exist in the water anyway, and that the discharge of nitrates from agricultural sources makes a significant contribution to the overall concentration of nitrates. However, just because there is a higher concentration of nitrates in the water bordering the land does not automatically mean that the landowner added to that concentration. Therefore, the principle of proportionality can be rebutted, and the polluter who caused/contributed the most damage has to pay the most, and one who didn't contribute shouldn't have to pay.

Listening (page 92)
3 *Suggested answers*
  Name of client: Martin James
  Reasons for meeting/telephone call: Client has a problem with having to dispose of a faulty product
  Client's product details: 10,000 light-up teddy bears, 10,000 battery rechargers and 20,000 batteries
  Initial problem: Manufacturer used faulty glue, and bears' eyes came off
  Action already taken by client: 10,000 faulty products recalled from Ireland
  Client's current concern: How to dispose of the bears, batteries and chargers
  Matters discussed: Whether the Battery Directive applies to the product, and whether the WEEE and the RoHS Directives might apply; what the possible consequences might be if the Directives did apply
  Advice given: Felt it was likely that the Directives might apply, but explained that the situation was unclear. Explained that more time was needed to research the matter further and suggested a further meeting.
  Activities agreed to be undertaken by the client: To make an appointment for the following week to meet and discuss the matter further
  Activities agreed to be undertaken by lawyer: None

Exam practice
Reading
1 I   2 D   3 A   4 C   5 H   6 F   7 E   8 B
Listening
1 C   2 C   3 A   4 B   5 B

Glossary

Sale of goods / Supplies of services

encumbrances *(n.)* claims which may exist over goods and which may lessen the value of the goods

exclusion *(n.pl.)* **(of terms)** where terms are either expressly or by implication not included in the contract for the sale of goods

express terms *(n.pl.)* terms that are specifically mentioned in the contract for the sale of goods

fitness for purpose *(n.)* that the goods are of merchantable quality and are fit for the purpose for which they are normally sold

goods *(n.pl.)* anything that is the subject of trade, manufacture or merchandise

guarantee *(n.)* any written statement supplied by a manufacturer indicating service or repair of goods for a period of time

hire purchase *(n.)* a method of buying goods so that they are paid for over a period of time; there is usually an agreement with a finance house

implied terms *(n.pl.)* terms that are in the contract by virtue of operation of law or dealings between the parties

implied undertaking as to title *(n.)* an implied condition that the seller has the right to sell the goods

merchantable quality *(n.)* that the goods are of a reasonable standard, taking into account the price and the purpose of the goods

misleading statements *(n.pl.)* incorrect verbal or written statements about goods

seller's lien *(n.)* a seller's lien or right to retain goods that have not been paid for, for the price unpaid while he is in possession of them

passing the title in goods *(n.)* moving ownership of the goods to the person who has paid for them

quiet possession of goods *(n.)* when the person who buys goods is entitled to enjoy them without interference from the previous owner or any other person who is interested in the goods

reservation of title *(n.)* where the seller retains the title to the goods sold (usually until the full price has been paid for the goods)

retention of title *(n.)* where the supplier of goods retains the contractual right to take back the goods he supplies to protect himself from the purchaser's insolvency

trade description *(n.)* any statement direct/indirect relating to goods

Negotiable instruments

accrue *(v.)* to accumulate, to increase

bill of exchange *(n.)* written and signed unconditional order, signed by three parties, directing the person who receives it to pay a fixed sum of money to a third party at a later date

bona-fide purchaser for value *(n.)* holder of a negotiable instrument who has received it in good faith

cheque *(n.)* negotiable instrument directing payment to a specific person at a specific time from funds held on deposit

drawer *(n.)* person who draws down funds

drawee *(n.)* person or financial institution that is directed to pay out the funds

draw up *(v.)* to prepare a legal document

endorsement *(n.)* signature which has the effect of legally transferring the negotiable instrument to the holder

interest *(n.)* money paid by a borrower for the money borrowed

instrument *(n.)* document evidencing or related to a form of security

negotiable *(adj.)* ability to be sold or legally given to another party as a form of payment by means of delivery or by endorsement (by signature on the document)

negotiable instrument *(n.)* signed document which can be transferred to another party and which contains a promise to pay the holder a sum of money at a future date or when demanded

principal *(n.)* **1** amount borrowed from a lender before interest is added **2** party to a transaction

promissory note *(n.)* promise in writing to repay a debt which sets out the terms of repayment

value *(n.)* worth

Secured transactions

fixed charge *(n.)* form of non-transferable non-possessory security which is realizable when the object of the security is transferred

floating charge *(n.)* charge over the assets of the debtor which becomes enforceable when the debtor defaults

lien *(n.)* form of legal claim over an asset which is used to secure a loan and which has to be discharged when the asset is sold

loan *(n.)* amount of money borrowed on terms and conditions

security *(n.)* something non-transferable, given as a guarantee of future repayment of a debt

Legal Latin

ab initio from the very beginning: *A contract is void **ab initio** if one of the parties is under age when the contract is entered into.*

bona fide in good faith: *As far as the party was concerned, the contract was **bona fide** and he had no reason to suspect the goods were stolen.*

caveat emptor let the buyer beware; used commercially to indicate the buyer's responsibility to check the quality of a purchase before buying

prima facie on the face of it: *The judge decided there was a **prima facie** case to answer.*

pro rata in proportion: *When new shares are issued, shareholders with pre-emption rights must be offered a percentage of the new shares **pro rata** to their shareholding.*

quorum minimum numbers of members required: *There was no **quorum**, so the meeting was postponed.*

res judicata a matter already decided: *The court refused to allow the lawyer to bring a fresh application on the matter as it was **res judicata**.*

ultra vires beyond/outside the powers: *The directors were acting **ultra vires** the Articles of Association when the company started selling soap, as the Articles only allowed the company to sell fish.*

verbatim word by word: *The lawyer quoted **verbatim** from the clause in the contract.*

versus against: *When the case of Jones v Smith was called in court, the registrar said 'Jones **versus** Smith'.*